Discovering Architecture with Activities and Games

I KNOW THAT BUILDING!

Jane D'Alelio

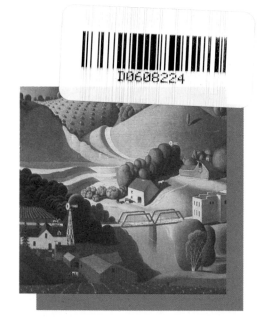

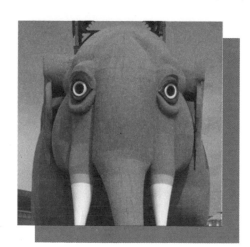

The Preservation Press

The Preservation Press
National Trust for Historic Preservation
1785 Massachusetts Avenue, N.W.
Washington, D.C. 20036

The National Trust for Historic Preservation in the United States is the
only private, nonprofit organization chartered by Congress to encourage
public participation in the preservation of sites, buildings and objects
significant in American history and culture. Support is provided by
membership dues, endowment funds, contributions and grants from federal
agencies, including the U.S. Department of the Interior, under the
provisions of the National Historic Preservation Act of 1966. The
opinions expressed here do not necessarily reflect the views or policies
of the Interior Department. For information about membership in the
National Trust, write to the above address.

Printed in the United States of America
96 95 94 93 92 91 90 89 5 4 3 2 1

Library of Congress Cataloging in Publication Data

D'Alelio, Jane.
    I know that building!: discovering architecture with activities and
games / Jane D'Alelio.

    p.   cm.
    Summary: Thirty projects for developing a better understanding of architecture.
    ISBN: 0-89133-133-6 (pbk.) : $14.95

    1. Architecture—Juvenile literature.   [1. Architecture.]   I. Title.
NA2555.D35 1989
720—dc19   87-36013

Edited by Diane Maddex, director, and Janet Walker, managing editor, The Preservation
Press

Designed by Jane D'Alelio, Ice House Graphics, Delaplane, Va.

Composed in ITC Zapf by Carver Publishing Services, Arlington, Va.

Color separations by Palace Press, Singapore

Printed on 90-pound Scott index by the John D. Lucas Printing Company, Baltimore, Md.

Acknowledgments

Books—like buildings—don't just
happen: they're planned and built by
many people working together. The
author expresses heartfelt thanks to
these talented people who provided
help and encouragement for *I Know
That Building!*: Pat Downey, Wendy
Cortesi, Diane Maddex, Janet Walker
and Elsie Hennig. Thanks go also to
Mary Thompson, Elizabeth
Hambrick, Dan Banks, Matthew
Brockel, Pamela Trible, Auriel Rundle
and Howard Paine.

Jane D'Alelio of Delaplane, Va., has
designed many children's activities
and materials for the National Geo-
graphic's *World* magazine, the National Wildlife Federation and the
National Zoo. Her design firm, Ice
House Graphics, also designs and
produces a variety of publications for
associations as well as other pub-
lishers.

Preface

Buildings, buildings, buildings—they're everywhere. Whether you live in the city, the country or in between, you can't miss them. In fact, you couldn't live without them, because buildings provide the basic shelter that all people need to survive. The design of buildings is called architecture, and much architecture provides not only shelter but beauty and fun as well.

This book is all about buildings—architecture—inside and out, tall and short, alone and in groups, old and new. Most of the activities in this book involve buildings that are old, because that is the special concern of the National Trust for Historic Preservation, the publisher. The National Trust helps people save old buildings and places all around the country. Just because a building is old doesn't mean that it can't continue to be used. Actually, today many people prefer to live and work in old buildings, because these places are often more interesting than new buildings.

Wouldn't *you* find it fun to live in or visit an old house with a long, winding banister that you could slide down? Or climb to the top of a tall, candy-striped lighthouse to see how the light works? Or buy a frankfurter at a stand shaped like a hot dog in a bun? Maybe you can still do some of these things at places near you. If not, at least you can picture yourself doing them in the architectural adventures that follow.

The archi-ventures in this book will show you what architecture is all about—how buildings are designed, who creates them, where the models for certain structures come from, how buildings have changed over the years. The activities also will tell you about some important American architects and some architectural styles that have been popular. As an extra, you can also learn about what goes on inside buildings (such as what furnishings were used) and outside (such as why gardens are important). You'll even be able to try your own hand at construction, putting together models of a one-room school, two skyscrapers and an old covered bridge. And just as important, you'll have a chance to become a preservationist—to help save some nice old buildings by taking a neighborhood survey, choosing a new building for an old Main Street and preserving a historic firehouse that can be reused for . . . what would you suggest?

When you are finished with the projects and games here, you will be on your way to discovering architecture. You should soon be able to say not just, "I know that building" but also, "I *like* that building!"

Diane Maddex and Janet Walker
Editors

Contents

Building with nature	4
Who settled where?	6
Voices from the past	8
History mystery	10
How houses change	14
Picture this	15
A-mazing landmarks	16
Block by block	18
Down on the farm	20
Watch out for ducks!	22
What does your garden say?	24
An architectural rebus	26
I'm sign smart	27
Morris was more than a chair	28
Music for the eyes	29
Tools of the trade	30
Rise to great heights	32
Pieces of history	37
Dress up Queen Anne	39
Bring back Main Street	44
Star signs	46
Welcome to stencil craft	49
How to spot a gargoyle	51
Wooden wonders	54
Go build!	61
Going to school in 1862	69
Light work	76
Who'll save old No. 9?	79
Archi-venture	86
Credits	87
Answers	88
Rub a cover!	back cover

Building with nature

When people build structures, they often use
shapes and designs that
are found in nature. American architect Frank Lloyd Wright (1867–1959)
is one of the best-known architects
who used forms in nature to inspire
his buildings. Wright believed that
nature offered architects many ideas.
"What is style?" he asked. "Every

flower has it; every animal has it. . . ."
Tree roots, a spiraled, chambered
nautilus, folded hands and the way
flowers open all gave Wright ideas for
buildings. The best designs, he
thought, develop from within, so that
their form is matched to their func-
tion. Wright also used materials such
as wood, stone and concrete as natu-
rally as possible. He never covered

them up, to allow their own colors,
textures and qualities to be admired.

On this page are nine photographs
of objects that you might see at the
beach or in a garden. On the opposite page are nine structures that architects, engineers and artists have
designed. Can you match these built
objects with their look-alikes in the
natural world?

Four-leaf clover

Sea gull

Sea urchin

Onions

Nautilus shell

Leaves

Daisy

Starfish

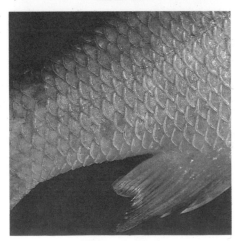
Fish scales

On each numbered line, write the name of the natural object that looks like the example with that number.

1. _____

2. _____

3. _____

4. _____

5. _____

6. _____

7. _____

8. _____

9. _____

1. Sports dome

2. Tie rod

3. Highway interchange

4. Cast-iron bridge

5. Airline terminal

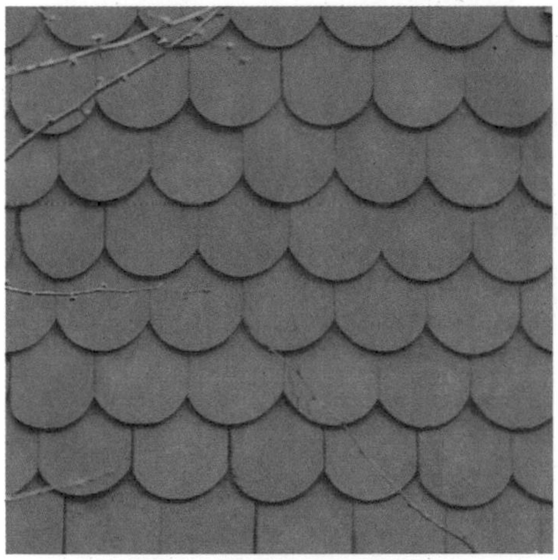

6. House shingles

7. Spiral staircase

8. Church dome

9. Stained-glass window

Who settled where?

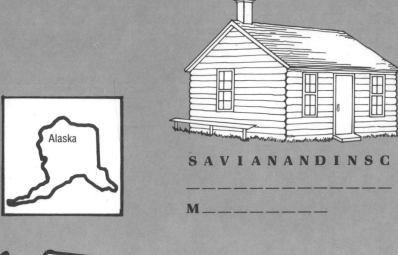

S A V I A N A N D I N S C

_ _ _ _ _ _ _ _ _ _ _ _

M _ _ _ _ _ _ _ _

People from many countries have built America. Some buildings that we think of as "American" really are based on styles that the settlers remembered from their homelands. When they began to build homes and towns here, immigrants had to use whatever materials were available, but they also mixed them with familiar construction techniques and building types.

Today, when we see a certain type of building, we often can tell the country or area its builder came from—its architectual roots. Try to identify which settlers built these buildings. The group's name is scrambled under each picture. Unscramble the letters and print the group in the first set of spaces. Then, in the second set of spaces, name a state in which these and similar buildings can be found. Here's a clue: the first letter of each state is already written in.

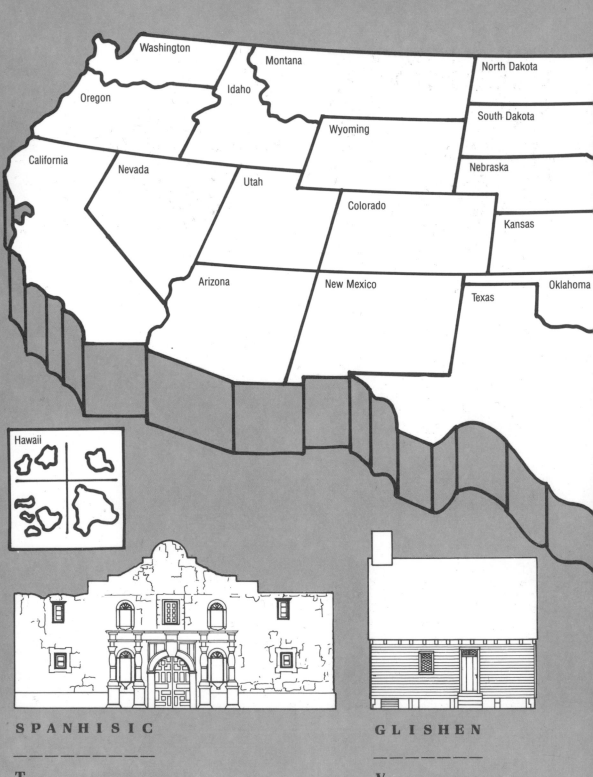

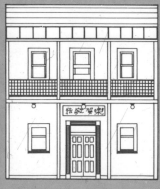

C H E E S I N

_ _ _ _ _ _ _

C _ _ _ _ _ _ _ _ _ _

S P A N H I S I C

_ _ _ _ _ _ _ _ _

T _ _ _ _ _

G L I S H E N

_ _ _ _ _ _ _

V _ _ _ _ _ _ _ _

In the 1890s large numbers of people from the western Ukraine, now part of the Union of Soviet Socialist Republics, settled in North Dakota as well as in Canada. They brought with them a distinctive style of building churches. This one, Josaphat Ukrainian Catholic Church (c. 1890s) in Gorham, N.D., has a typical onion dome.

N A M E R I C A
S D I N N I A

_ _ _ _ _ _ _ _ _
_ _ _ _ _ _ _ _ _
O _ _ _ _ _ _ _ _

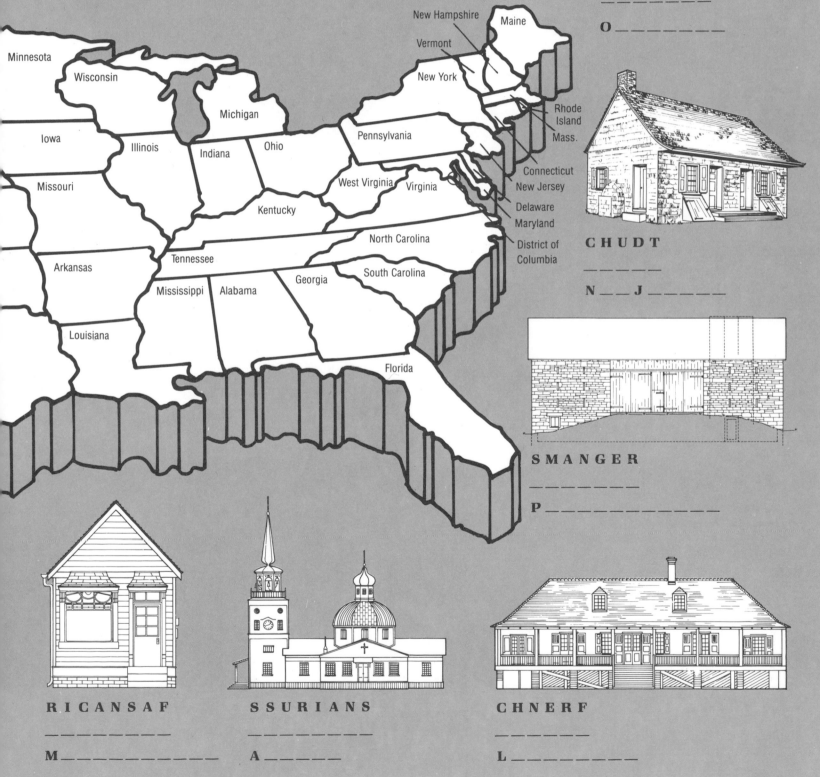

C H U D T

_ _ _ _ _ _
N _ _ J _ _ _ _ _

S M A N G E R

_ _ _ _ _ _ _ _
P _ _ _ _ _ _ _ _ _ _ _

R I C A N S A F

_ _ _ _ _ _ _ _ _
M _ _ _ _ _ _ _ _ _

S S U R I A N S

_ _ _ _ _ _ _ _
A _ _ _ _ _ _

C H N E R F

_ _ _ _ _ _
L _ _ _ _ _ _ _

7

Voices from the past

For many centuries, Americans have built buildings in which to live, go to school, work and have fun. Over the years, the styles of these buildings have changed, as have their materials, sizes and ways in which they are built. But even though these things change, people still need somewhere to live, go to school, work and play.

Let's take a trip back in time to find out more about how buildings looked during four eras in American history. Listen to the voices of 16 young people talk about the buildings that were important in their lives. Read and match their words with each of the 16 buildings here. Write the number of the building after the correct quotation.

How would you describe the buildings in your life? How do they look compared to these buildings?

❝The wooden building in which I went to school in 1890 later became a branch bank.❞ ☐

❝On Sundays my parents took me to the park so we could listen to Sousa marches.❞ ☐

❝Our house looked like it had two front doors. Actually, the one on the right was the entrance to a side passageway.❞ ☐

❝I remember two things about my cousin's business. The first was its beautiful wrought-iron balcony. The second was the constant aroma of bread baking.❞ ☐

❝On summer days I would go out to the country to watch the sails turning. Once the miller let me climb up a narrow stairway to the cap.❞ ☐

Home	School

1. Sandgates on Cat Creek **2. Chancellor Avenue School**

1700–1800

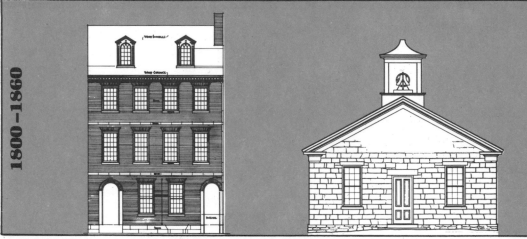

5. Baltimore town house **6. Stone School**

1800–1860

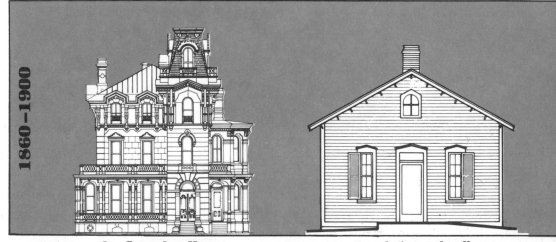

9. Goyer-Lee House **10. Broad River Schoolhouse**

1860–1900

13. Martin Avenue house **14. Portola Valley School**

1900 on

Work	Play

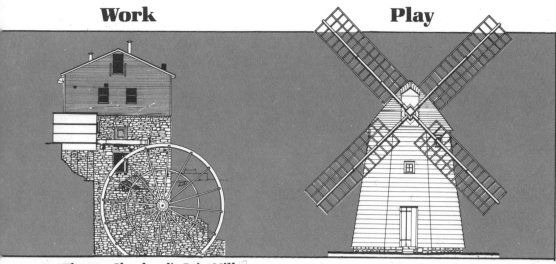

3. Thomas Shepherd's Grist Mill | 4. Long Island windmill

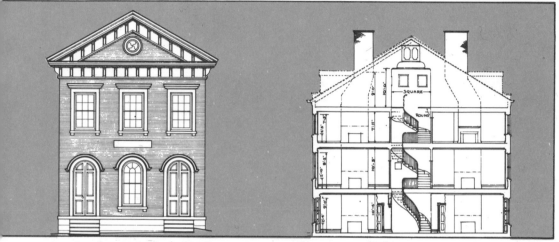

7. Southport Savings Bank | 8. New York row house

11. Lundberg Bakery | 12. Tower Grove Park Bandstand

15. Silver King Ore Loading Station | 16. Carnegie Library

"At the company that my father managed, ore from the mine was loaded into railroad cars that pulled in below the storage floor." ☐

"Because of the threat of fires, my house in Maryland had chimneys at each end rather than in the middle." ☐

"My school in California looked a lot like the old Spanish missions nearby." ☐

"One of my favorite things to do when I was young was to read books in a building whose dome made it look as important as a state capitol." ☐

"I remember the day the cobblestones arrived for our bungalow in California. We even covered the four front columns with them." ☐

"All my school years were spent in a little stone school with two windows in front and a bell that called us to class." ☐

"My family owned a grist mill with a huge wrought-iron water wheel. We worked hard to grind wheat into flour for all our neighbors." ☐

"When I visited my cousins in the city, what fun we had sliding all the way down the polished stair banister!" ☐

"My favorite room in our house was way up on the fourth floor under the mansard roof. I could look out at the little balconies." ☐

"The first school in our town was a one-room stone schoolhouse. On top of the bell tower was a fancy wrought-iron weathervane." ☐

"When I began to work there as a teller in 1855, I thought that the round window in the gable looked like a shiny new penny." ☐

Where are we?

History mystery

Like detectives solving a crime, archeologists look for clues from the past. Can you solve this mystery?

Evidence of the past is all around us . . . in our backyards, down the block, across town and across the country. Here's a history mystery for you to figure out: Imagine that you and your family find yourselves in a different part of the United States during a winter vacation. Hiking in strange territory, you climb a hill and suddenly come across the puzzling sight above. You decide to investigate this ghost town. As you approach the structures, you hear nothing. You feel the hot sun beating down on you but catch a hint of a breeze.

Carefully examine the scene above. Then answer the following questions, circling the correct answers.

1. **What is the temperature?**
   30°F 50°F 90°F

2. **How much rain falls here each month?**
   Less than 1" 10" 30"

3. **What types of plants live here?**
   trees shrubs grasses

4. **What types of buildings were constructed here?**
   hotels stores factories

5. **Where are you?**
   desert prairie rain forest

6. **What part of the United States is this?**
   northeastern southern western

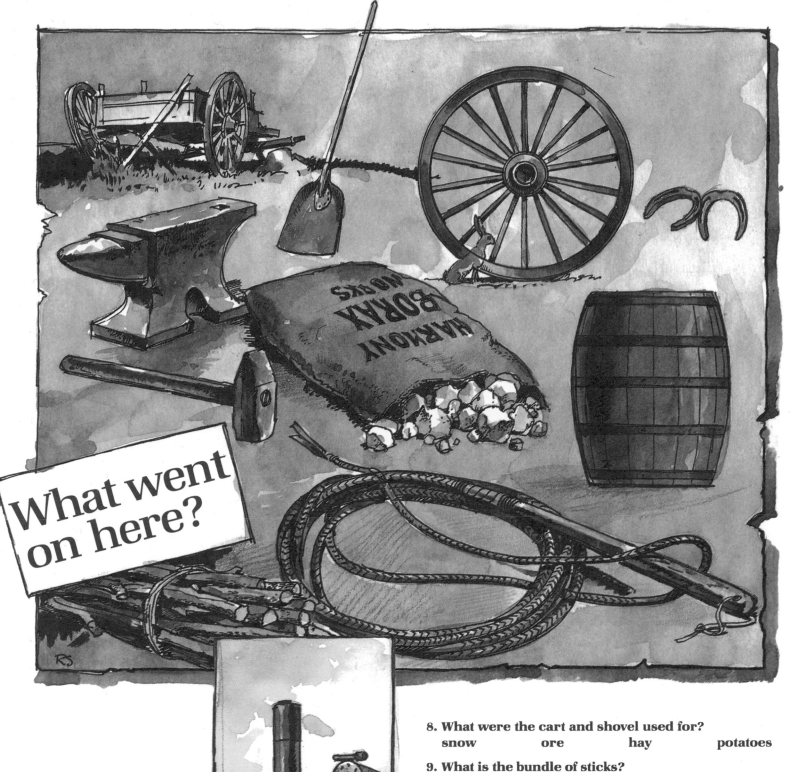

What went on here?

As you walk into the ruins, you notice many things that were left behind at the site. The clues above will help you discover what happened here. Circle the correct answers below and at right.

7. The structure in the picture above has ashes in the lower part and a pipe for smoke or steam. What is this?
pizza oven   boiler and furnace   barbecue

8. What were the cart and shovel used for?
snow   ore   hay   potatoes

9. What is the bundle of sticks?
corn stalks   shrub branches   bamboo poles

10. The sticks were used as what?
fuel for a fire   food for animals   toys for children

11. The wheel is seven feet tall. To what was it attached?
large wagon   pony cart   bicycle

12. Who used the hammer and anvil?
carpenter   blacksmith   painter

13. What pulled the cart?
tractor   people   horses or mules

14. Remembering clues about the climate, what did the barrel hold?
water   oil   maple syrup

15. What is in the burlap bag?
coal   borax   diamonds

Who used these?

As you sift through some sand you find an old leather bag containing a treasure trove of personal belongings. Examine the picture above and answer the questions to help you decide who used these items.

16. **Who left the bottle, tin can, knife and piece of a bowl?**
    cook magician plumber

17. **Who used the eyeglasses and the ledger pages?**
    horse trader farmer clerk

18. **When was the food (victuals) ordered?**
    1788 1886 1980

19. **What country did the owner of the coins and postcard come from?**
    China France Italy

20. **From the address on the postcard, you probably are in which state?**
    Maine Ohio California

21. **What piece of clothing did the buttons come from?**
    bathing suits dresses work clothes

22. **From what you have learned, what was this ghost town?**
    ski resort military fort mining camp

Fill in the blanks

Now, fill in the blanks, making sure the numbers of the answers below correspond to the numbers of your circled answers.

You already know quite a lot about this mysterious area. Because the temperature is (1) _____ in the winter and there is little vegetation other than (3) _____, you must be in the (5) _____. So little rain falls, (2) _____ each month, you don't see forests or green fields. You know from the postcard you are in the state of (20) _____, which is in the (6) _____ part of the United States. The buildings you see were part of a (22) _____ _____ where (15) _____, a mineral used in cleaning products, was put into burlap bags. (13) _____ pulled huge wagons with heavy loads through the desert. A (12) _____ _____ made sure that their hooves were well protected. A (14) _____ barrel was probably taken along on the journeys. Quite a few people lived and worked here. A (16) _____ prepared meals, and a (17) _____ working in a company office ordered supplies and kept track of wages. Some of the workers were from (19) _____. This camp was operating in (18) _____.

How borax was made

Did you guess the answers? The photograph above shows one of the famous 20-mule teams that carried borax 165 miles across the desert and over the mountains from Death Valley to the nearest railroad junction in the community of Mohave, Calif.

The old Harmony Borax Works opened in 1883 in Death Valley, Calif. Workers, many of them Chinese, dug the ore from the ground, shoveling it onto sleds and carts, which took it to the nearby processing plant. There, a large boiler, fueled by mesquite and other desert shrubs, heated water to dissolve the mineral and separate it from impurities. The liquid then went into cooling vats—huge tanks where the borax crystallized on pieces of metal. When it dried, it could be broken off into chunks and loaded into bags for shipment.

Each 20-mule team made the 30-day round trip from the mining camp to the rail line pulling two loaded wagons and a water tank. Even when they were empty, the giant wagons weighed almost four tons each. The front wheels stood five feet tall, and the rear wheels were seven feet. The 20-mule team stretched 100 feet in front of the driver, who guided the animals with a thin cotton rope, called a jerk line.

The Harmony plant closed down about 100 years ago. Today, you can see the preserved ruins—now a state historic landmark—near the little town of Furnace Creek, Calif., part of Death Valley National Monument.

SOFTENS WATER SAVES CLEANS AND WHITENS CLOTHES

20 MULE TEAM PACKAGE BORAX FOR SALE HERE

Borax today

The 20-mule teams no longer rumble across the desert with their heavy loads, but you can see their picture in the supermarket on products containing borax.

This 1906 poster advertises borax for household washing. Today, borax is found in many other products such as fire retardant chemicals, fertilizers, glass, fiberglass, porcelain enamel on appliances, plastics, ceramic glazes, cosmetics, medicines (including boric acid) and other household and industrial products.

Borax is still mined at two locations in California, one of them not far from Death Valley. Modern machinery has replaced the picks and shovels of the Harmony plant. Together, these mines produce about 62 percent of the world's supply of this valuable mineral, which has been useful for so long.

How houses change

n the past, houses were built to last. With good care, they can last for many families to live in. Since this Gothic Revival–style house was built more than 100 years ago, many changes have been made. Find 12 changes and write them in the numbered spaces.

1. _____
2. _____
3. _____
4. _____
5. _____
6. _____
7. _____
8. _____
9. _____
10. _____
11. _____
12. _____

14

Picture this

This house was torn down 80 years ago, but old photographs such as the ones here are important because they show how people lived in the past. Although the family is not present, we can tell a lot about their household from the photographs. Find and check off eight activities that the family could have done here in 1900:

Watered the plants

Played the piano

Watched television

Operated a computer

Rocked a baby

Played an electric guitar

Read a book

Served tea

Set the grandfather clock

Slid down the banister

Lighted the lamps

Talked on the telephone

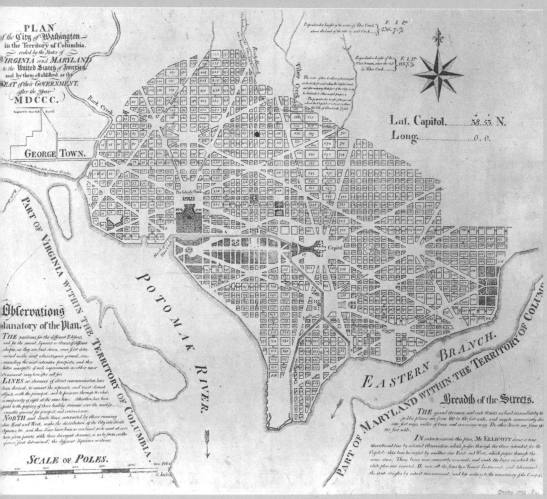

A-mazing landmarks

Today, Washington, D.C., is one of the world's most beautiful capital cities. But in 1790, when President George Washington selected the site to be the capital of the United States, it did not have any of the wide avenues or important buildings that can be found now. President Washington asked a French engineer, Pierre Charles L'Enfant, to plan the city in 1791. L'Enfant drew up a plan of square blocks (a grid), which were crossed with diagonal avenues named for the states. Can you tell from L'Enfant's plan at left where he wanted to place the White House and the Capitol? After L'Enfant left Washington, surveyor Andrew Ellicott completed the plan.

Find your way around Washington by looking for the 12 landmarks below. Read the addresses in the captions, locate them on the modern city map and mark each landmark's number in the circle on the map.

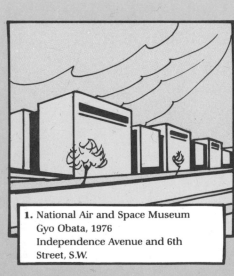

1. National Air and Space Museum
Gyo Obata, 1976
Independence Avenue and 6th
Street, S.W.

2. Andrew Jackson Statue
Clark Mills, 1853
Pennsylvania Avenue and 16th
Street, N.W.

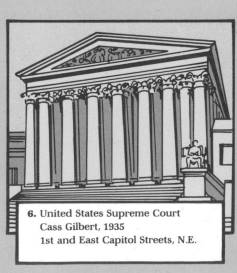

3. White House
James Hoban and
Benjamin Latrobe, 1792
1600 Pennsylvania Avenue, N.W.

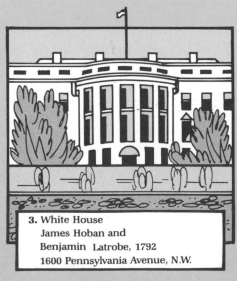

4. Martin Luther King Memorial Library
Ludwig Mies van der Rohe, 1972
G Street between 9th and 10th
Streets, N.W.

5. Washington Monument
Robert Mills, 1848–85
15th Street between Constitution
and Independence Avenues, N.W.

6. United States Supreme Court
Cass Gilbert, 1935
1st and East Capitol Streets, N.E.

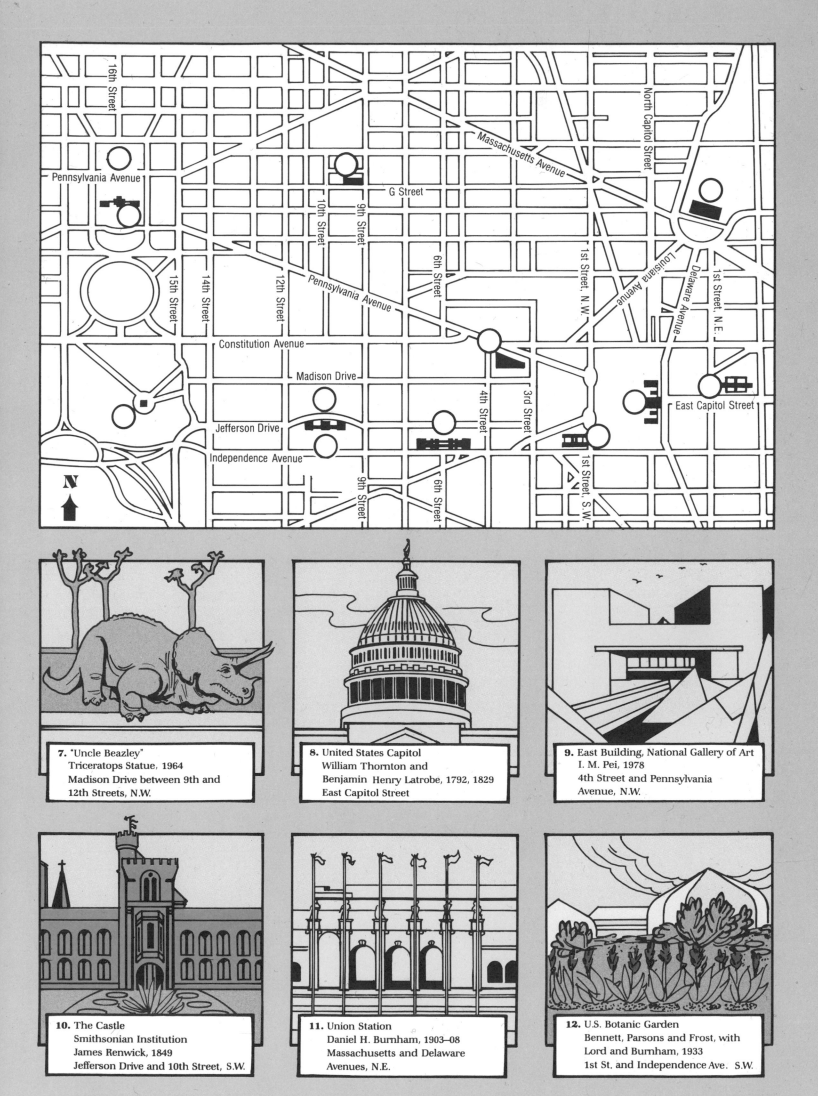

7. "Uncle Beazley"
Triceratops Statue, 1964
Madison Drive between 9th and
12th Streets, N.W.

8. United States Capitol
William Thornton and
Benjamin Henry Latrobe, 1792, 1829
East Capitol Street

9. East Building, National Gallery of Art
I. M. Pei, 1978
4th Street and Pennsylvania
Avenue, N.W.

10. The Castle
Smithsonian Institution
James Renwick, 1849
Jefferson Drive and 10th Street, S.W.

11. Union Station
Daniel H. Burnham, 1903–08
Massachusetts and Delaware
Avenues, N.E.

12. U.S. Botanic Garden
Bennett, Parsons and Frost, with
Lord and Burnham, 1933
1st St. and Independence Ave. S.W.

Block by block

One way to find historic buildings and places that should be preserved is to survey a block, a neighborhood or a whole town. People conducting a survey note a building's features and describe its importance. Conduct your own survey. For each building shown, circle the box in each of the six categories that looks most like the building above the form.

Mel's Diner (c. 1930), Queens, N.Y.

Kuntz House (c. 1890), Louisville, Ky.

FUNCTION	Restaurant	Home	Meeting place	Church	Restaurant	Home	Meeting place	Church
ENTRANCE STYLE	Victorian	Gothic Revival	Moderne	Vernacular	Victorian	Gothic Revival	Moderne	Vernacular
EXTERIOR MATERIAL	Stone	Wood	Metal	Brick	Stone	Wood	Metal	Brick
WINDOW DESIGN	Transom	Plate glass	Stained glass	2-over-2	Transom	Plate glass	Stained glass	2-over-2
ROOF SHAPE	End gable	Side gable	Curvilinear	End gable	End gable	Side gable	Curvilinear	End gable
SPECIAL FEATURE	Bell tower	Vent cap	Lintel	Lunette	Bell tower	Vent cap	Lintel	Lunette

An architectural survey to do

Odd Fellows Hall (1875), Idaho City, Idaho

Grace Church (1867), Washington, D.C.

FUNCTION	Restaurant	Home	Meeting place	Church
ENTRANCE STYLE	Victorian	Gothic Revival	Moderne	Vernacular
EXTERIOR MATERIAL	Stone	Wood	Metal	Brick
WINDOW DESIGN	Transom	Plate glass	Stained glass	2-over-2
ROOF SHAPE	End gable	Side gable	Curvilinear	End gable
SPECIAL FEATURE	Bell tower	Vent cap	Lintel	Lunette

Down on the farm

Stone City, Iowa, by Grant Wood (1892–1942).

Down on the **farm,** the house where the farm family lives is just one of many important buildings. Other farm structures are called outbuildings and come in all shapes and sizes. They store crops for future use, house animals and protect equipment and **water** supplies.

People living on farms once depended almost entirely on themselves for all their needs. They did everything from growing most of their own food to making feather pillows from their own **ducks.** Outbuildings helped them with these tasks. Horses, used to pull **plows** and wagons before the **tractor** became common, lived in a **barn** or stable. Birdhouses attracted insect-eating birds. Most farms relied on a natural spring or a well for water. A springhouse not only enclosed the place where water bubbled up out of the ground, it also kept cans of **milk** cold in its channel of running water; a well house covered the well and kept people from falling in. An icehouse stored ice underground to keep foods cold and provide frosty drinks for hard workers in the summer. High on stilts or pipes to keep away mice and rats, a corncrib held ears of dried feed corn. **Grain** for **cows** was stored in a silo. A wagon shed protected farm equipment from the weather.

Today's farmers need fewer outbuildings, but they often maintain these old buildings for other uses. Many of the outbuildings shown on the opposite page can still be found today. To complete the word find, locate all the words above in dark type as well as those under the buildings. Draw a line around each word you find. The words may go up or down, straight across or diagonally in any direction.

STABLE

BIRDHOUSE

ICEHOUSE

WAGON SHED

CORNCRIB

WELL HOUSE

```
C O R N C R I B W B A
H Y S O Z B C I A F N
I E W M S A E R G S S
C S O I P R H D O K P
K U L L E N O H N C R
E O P K S T U O S U I
N H E P U R S U H D N
H G H P O A E S E U G
O O S N H C T E D R H
U D R G L T Z O A Q O
S K D S L O E I N P U
E W A T E R N K S A S
F A R M W S T A B L E
```

DOGHOUSE

CHICKEN HOUSE

SILO

SPRINGHOUSE

Watch out for ducks!

When is a duck not a duck? When it's a whale, an orange or a hot dog, that's when. The "ducks" we're talking about are funny-shaped structures that often look like the items sold inside or the name of their business. These structures were designed to call attention to themselves, so they act like their own signs. You can find them along old highways and in other out-of-the way places.

Lucy the Elephant, Margate, N.J. ☐   **Benewah Dairy No. 1, Spokane, Wash.** ☐

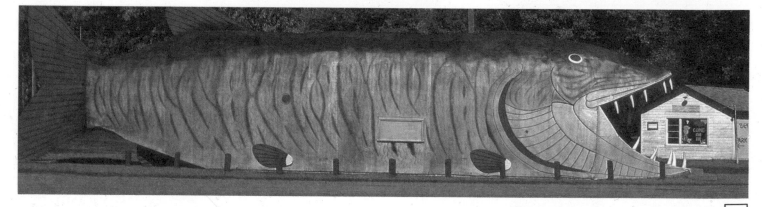

Big Fish Supper Club, Bena, Minn. ☐

Rhymes to match

Play a game of ducks by matching the rhymes below with the structures. Write the rhyme number in the box next to each picture.

1. Oh where, oh where has my little dog gone?
Oh where, oh where can he be?
With his ears cut short and his tail cut long.
Oh where, oh where can he be?

2. Oranges and lemons
Say the bells of St. Clements.

3. I'm a little teapot
short and stout.
Here is my handle.
Here is my spout.

4. Milkman, Milkman, where have you been?
In buttermilk channel up to my chin.
I spilt my milk and I spoilt my clothes
and got a long icicle hung from my nose.

5. Simple Simon went a fishing
For to catch a whale.
All the water he had got
Was in his mother's pail.

6. Way down South where bananas grow,
A grasshopper stepped on an elephant's toe.
The elephant said, with tears in his eyes,
"Pick on somebody your own size."

7. One, two, three, four, five,
I caught a fish alive.
Why did you let him go?
'Cause he bit my finger so.

Orange Julep, Plattsburgh, N.Y. ☐

Bob's Java Jive, Tacoma, Wash. ☐

Tail o' the Pup, North Hollywood, Calif. ☐

Whale Car Wash, Oklahoma City, Okla. ☐

Famous Big Duck migrates to new nest

The namesake of all the little ducks shown there is the Big Duck, which was built in Riverhead, Long Island, N.Y., in 1931. This area of Long Island was famous for its roasting ducks. Martin Maurer raised a lot of ducks for sale and decided that a big duck would be a good place to sell them because it would attract big crowds. His stucco-cov-

ered duck was designed by William Collins. It stands 15 feet high and weighs about 10 tons. In 1941 it was moved, and then the land on which it sat was sold. The owners donated it to the county for use as a museum. But first it had to be moved again.

The Big Duck was relocated on a flatbed truck in 1988 to a temporary resting place while its new home was prepared. To help out, a Big Duck Preservation Fund was created for donations of money.

The Big Duck is so famous that it appeared on the cover of *The New Yorker* magazine. Other ducks do not receive so much attention. (Architects Robert Venturi, Denise Scott Brown and Steven Izenour coined the name "duck" to mean any oddly shaped structure.) Many of them were built 50 years ago and have been abandoned because new highways bypassed them. They can use friends too. Watch out for ducks near your home.

What does your garden say?

Victorians who lived during the middle and end of the 19th century loved flowers and gardening. Their homes and public buildings often were landscaped with flower beds arranged in carefully planned patterns and colors. Some flower gardens looked like bands of colored ribbon, while others resembled exotic Oriental carpets.

Victorians also liked to communicate with flowers. How did they do this? Certain flowers were given specific meanings. Dictionaries of the period even listed the meanings of flowers to help people send messages with their flowers, like a code.

Pretend that you lived in the Victorian era and collected a bouquet of white bellflowers, pink carnations and heliotrope for your mother. What did the flowers tell her? Use the list below to decipher the message and the occasion.

Alyssum, sweet	Worth beyond beauty	Holly	Good wishes
Bellflower, white	Gratitude	Morning glory	Farewell
Carnation, pink	Mother's Day	Rose, red	Passionate love
Cherry blossom	Education	Sunflower	Homage and devotion
Crocus	Youthful gladness	Violet	Steadfastness
Daisy	Innocence	Zinnia	Thoughts of absent friends
Heliotrope	Devotion		

In 1880 garden designer Peter Henderson recommended that gardeners plant flowers like the ones below to form a colorful Victorian pattern. His plan for this sample garden appears on the opposite page.

Re-create his design by using the photographs as a guide to color the garden plan. Find a crayon to match the color in each photograph. (In some cases, 20th-century varieties have been substituted for 19th-century flowers no longer available.)

**1. Cardinal flower
Blue**

**2. Joseph's coat
Yellow green**

**3. Bloodleaf
Maroon**

**4. Geranium
White**

**5. Golden Marguerite
Yellow orange**

**6. Geranium
Pink**

**7. Fountain plant
Gray green**

**8. Geranium
Red**

AN·ARCHITECTURAL·REBUS

My·gr 8 ·grand 🍐🐜· house· was· $BILL$ t· [inn]· 1845. It's·in·the· [dog] GRRR! [mouse] EEEK! ·

Rev [eye] val·st [eye] le·with·st 8 ly· [columns] ·

on·the·f [runner] t,·a· ▲ lar· pedi [cupcake] ·on·

[top] ·and·a· [cloud] ow· [witch] lets· [sun][lightbulb] ·

[inn] to·the·attic. Each· [column] ·has·a· [cards] ·

8 ive·carved· [cap] ital. Over·the·f [runner] t

d [ore box] ·is·a·transom· [cloud] ow. My·gr 8 ·

[graham cracker][?] ·house·is· [pail] ed·white·as· ❄ ·

·and·the· ‖ R ·black.

[can] U ·name·the·

p ❤❤ ·of· this·

[dog] GRRR! [mouse] EEEK! · Rev [eye]

val·house?

capital · pediment · attic window · column · transom window · shutter

I'm sign smart

Match the riddles with these old signs by putting the riddle number next to the right sign.

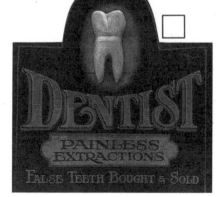

1. It's cool, sweet and yummy,
   A treat for every tummy.
   In crunchy cone or dish,
   Whichever way you wish.

2. I have a soul but not a heart,
   I have a tongue, but speak no part,
   I have an eye, but cannot see.
   On a foot is where I'll be.

3. It has a root, but not a leaf,
   It has a coat, but not a sleeve,
   It has a crown, but not a head.
   It shines so white in its pink bed.

4. My first is in Crimson, never in blue,
   My second's in Old, never in new,
   My third is in Land, not in sea,
   My fourth is in Apple—do you know me?

5. A flying red horse
   Upon a tall pole—
   If you're short of gas
   This may be your goal.

6. This place takes you back
   To treasures and bric-a-brac
   Like precious rings golden
   And other things olden.

7. Around the seas I sail
   In sunshine or in gale,
   And people tell the tale
   Of Jonah and the _____.

8. Gorgeous castle, magic house,
   Sleeping princess, giant mouse,
   Thrilling rides and marching band.
   Where's this wondrous world so grand?

9. The chorus of birds, how they sang,
   sang, sang.
   But all I could do was just bang,
   bang, bang.

27

Morris was more than a chair

Around the turn of the century, many Americans relaxed in their living rooms or parlors in what was called a Morris chair. These comfortable chairs had adjustable backs and removable cushions.

But who was Morris? William Morris (1834–96) was a British designer, writer and printer who led the Arts and Crafts movement. Morris and the other Arts and Crafts designers promoted work that looked handmade and used

examples from nature including plants and birds. They designed interior furnishings such as wallpapers, fabrics, carpets and stained glass in a distinctive, flowing style like the one here for you to color.

This design for a fabric cushion produced by Morris and Company is known as the "Rose Wreath." The Arts and Crafts style called for using soft, natural colors. Which colors will you choose for this Morris design?

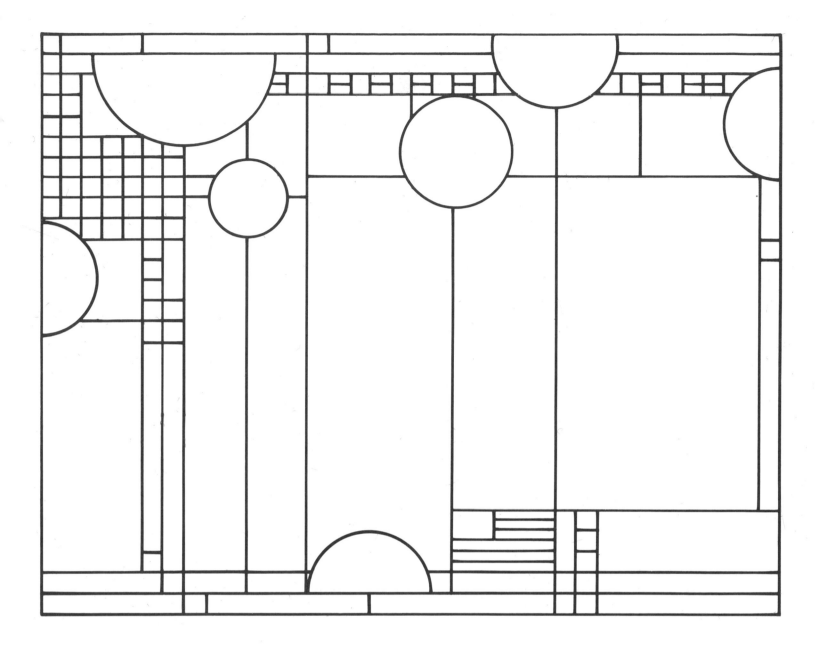

Music for the eyes: color it Wright

Did you know that architecture has been called frozen music? (Think of a beautiful building as a song held in time.) And, when buildings have colorful stained-glass windows, it's as if they are playing music for our eyes. The light shines through the bright colors and creates rainbows of patterns all around.

Stained glass is made up of many little pieces of glass held together with lead strips. The glass actually is colored when it is made rather than stained later. The art of making stained glass goes back to medieval days, when it was used in European cathedrals. Stained glass also can be found in homes and public buildings in patterns that include flowers, animals, people, places and abstract geometric shapes. Two famous American stained-glass designers were Louis Comfort Tiffany (1848–1923) and Frank Lloyd Wright (1867–1959).

This window for you to color was created by Wright in 1912 for the playhouse at the Avery Coonley House in Riverside, Ill. Will you choose the same colors that Frank Lloyd Wright did?

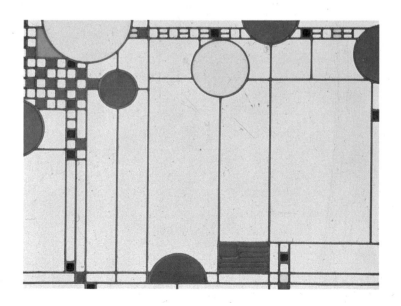

Tools of the trade

Buildings cannot be built or restored without craftspeople and tools. Different skills and different types of construction work all are needed to build a building in the first place or to bring it back to life so we can enjoy it.

Here is a puzzle to test your skills at identifying who does what task with which tool in a building. Six scrambled sets of construction trades are shown, with three pictures in each set. Select the three pictures that belong in each set by filling in the answers on the right.

Carve a gargoyle

Wood

Plasterer

Tongs

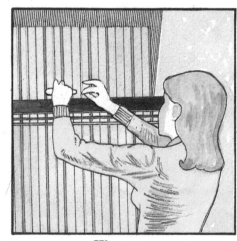

Weaver

Painter

Make curtains

Carpenter

Stone

Carpenters

What they use: _____

What they do: _____

Painters

What they use: _____

What they do: _____

Sculptors

What they use: _____

What they do: _____

Metalsmiths

What they use: _____

What they do: _____

Plasterers

What they use: _____

What they do: _____

Weavers

What they use: _____

What they do: _____

Sculptor

Paint

Build a staircase

Restore a molding

Metalsmith

Decorative mold

Fabric

Design a railing

Paint a wall

Rise to great heights

Frank Lloyd Wright wanted to build a mile-high building. This has not been tried yet, but the skyscrapers we do have are symbols of modern cities everywhere. The first ones were built in the late 19th century and seem small compared to today's giants. Skyscraper construction took off because tall, narrow buildings save land costs (and people like the way they look). But skyscrapers could not have been built if two things had not been developed: iron and steel frames (skeletons) and elevators.

Following this brief skyscraper history are two examples you can build yourself. All you need are scissors and glue or transparent tape.

Home Insurance Building (1885), Chicago. (Demolished.) Designed by William Le Baron Jenney. 10 stories, approximately 150 feet. One of the first forerunners of modern skyscrapers, this brick building was supported by an iron and steel frame.

Woolworth Building (1913), New York City. Designed by Cass Gilbert. 60 stories, 792 feet. Part of the second era of skyscraper construction, this landmark's shape and decoration recall older Gothic cathedrals. Called the Cathedral of Commerce, it is faced in terra cotta.

Empire State Building (1931), New York City. Designed by Shreve, Lamb and Harmon. 102 stories, 1,250 feet. This sleek tower, with its steplike setbacks typical of skyscrapers in the 1920s and 1930s, has long been a symbol of New York (the Empire State).

Seagram Building (1958), New York City. Designed by Ludwig Mies van der Rohe, with Philip Johnson. 38 stories, 525 feet. This amber glass and bronze International Style skyscraper has inspired imitations in almost every city.

American Telephone and Telegraph Company Building (1984), New York City. Designed by Philip Johnson, with John Burgee. 37 stories, 648 feet. The building is famous for its Chippendale-style pediment that makes it look like a piece of furniture.

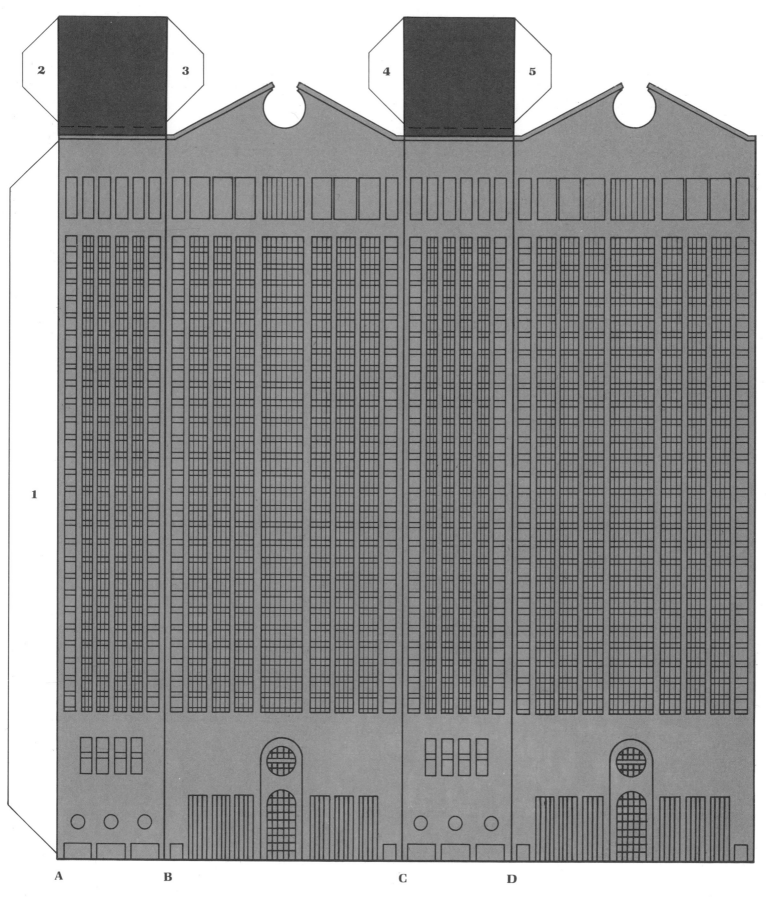

Build AT&T

Note: Before you make this model, read the instructions on the reverse side for the Woolworth Building. Then make that model first.

1. Cut out the entire building. Don't forget the tabs!

2. Cut out the hole in the Chippendale pediment.

3. Fold down tabs 1 through 5.

4. Fold the model into a rectangle at the darker lines.

5. Glue tab 1 to the inside back edge of side D.

6. Glue tab 2 to side D.

7. Glue tab 3 to side B.

8. Glue tab 4 to side B.

9. Glue tab 5 to side D.

Can you top this?

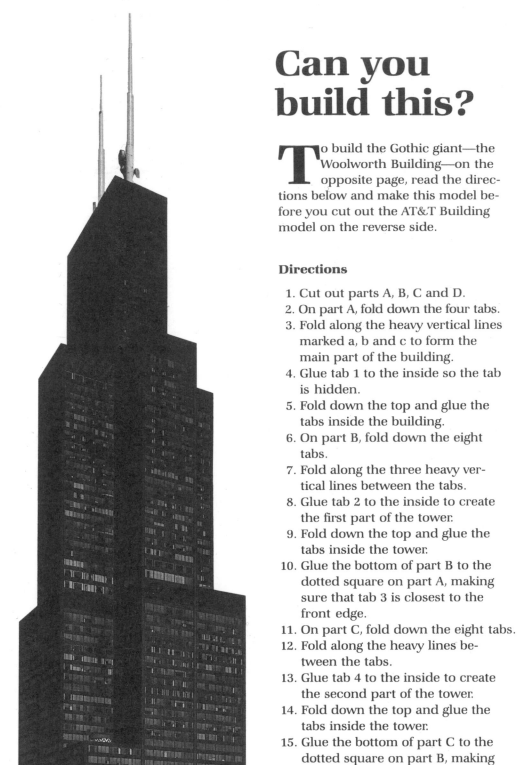

The tallest skyscraper in the world is the Sears Tower in Chicago (see the photograph at right). Designed by Skidmore, Owings and Merrill and completed in 1974, the building is 110 stories and 1,454 feet high.

No one really knows what the first American skyscraper was. Some historians think it was the Home Insurance Company Building (see page 32). Others believe it was the Equitable Life Assurance Company Building in New York City, built 15 years earlier in 1870. It was only five stories and 130 feet tall, but it had an elevator so that the upper floors could be fully used.

The Chicago Tribune Tower was designed based on an architectural competition in 1922 that brought in more than 200 entries from 23 countries. The winner was the firm of Howells and Hood. Skyscrapers today sometimes are still designed through competitions.

The outside walls are not what hold up a skyscraper. The steel skeleton framework inside provides the support for all the floors, people and furnishings in a tall building.

Can you build this?

To build the Gothic giant—the Woolworth Building—on the opposite page, read the directions below and make this model before you cut out the AT&T Building model on the reverse side.

Directions

1. Cut out parts A, B, C and D.
2. On part A, fold down the four tabs.
3. Fold along the heavy vertical lines marked a, b and c to form the main part of the building.
4. Glue tab 1 to the inside so the tab is hidden.
5. Fold down the top and glue the tabs inside the building.
6. On part B, fold down the eight tabs.
7. Fold along the three heavy vertical lines between the tabs.
8. Glue tab 2 to the inside to create the first part of the tower.
9. Fold down the top and glue the tabs inside the tower.
10. Glue the bottom of part B to the dotted square on part A, making sure that tab 3 is closest to the front edge.
11. On part C, fold down the eight tabs.
12. Fold along the heavy lines between the tabs.
13. Glue tab 4 to the inside to create the second part of the tower.
14. Fold down the top and glue the tabs inside the tower.
15. Glue the bottom of part C to the dotted square on part B, making sure that tab 5 is closest to the front edge.
16. On part D, fold down the nine tabs. Then fold the roof along the three heavy lines. Crease the four lines on the roof marked d.
17. Glue tabs 6 and 7 to the inside of the roof and building section. Glue the remaining side tabs to the inside to square up the form.
18. Glue the bottom of part D to the dotted square on part C.

And now you have topped off a Gothic giant!

A Gothic giant

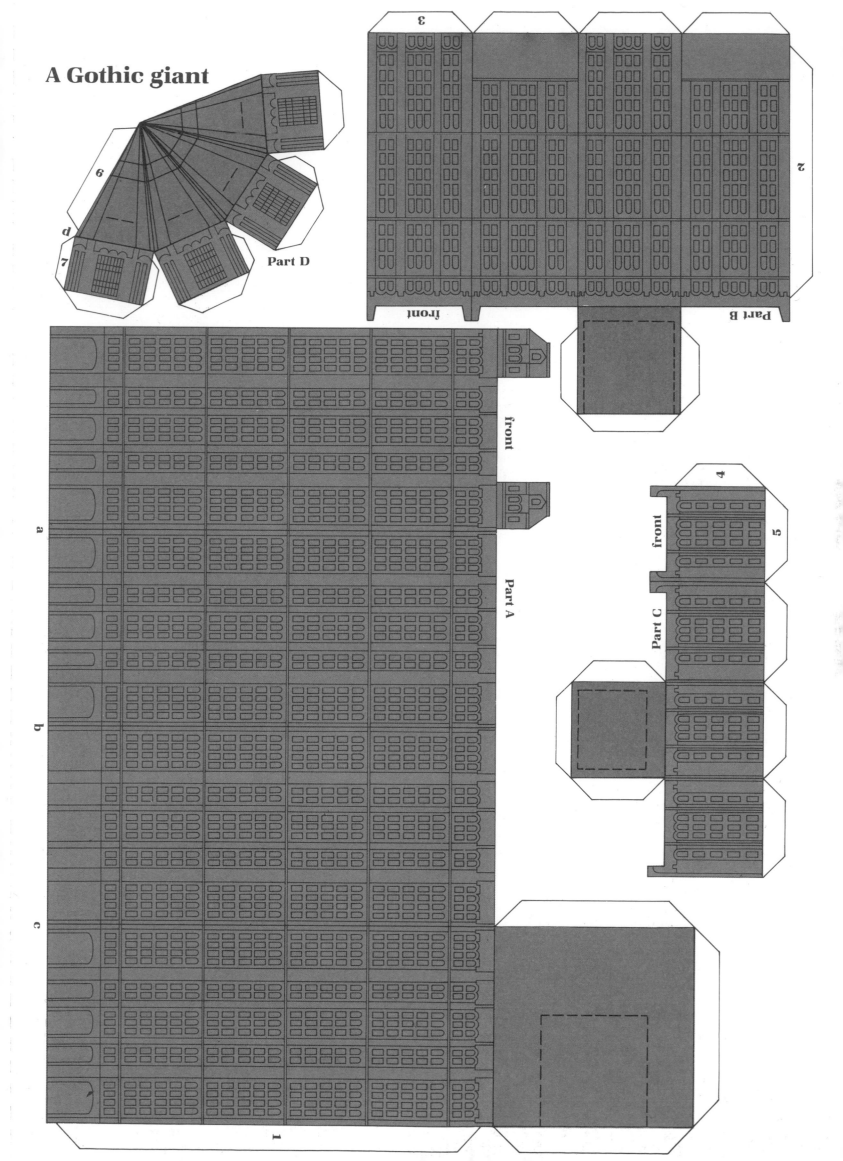

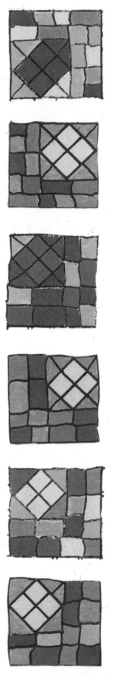

Pieces of history

For thousands of years people all over the world have used mosaics—designs made with tiny pieces of glass or stone—to decorate their walls and floors. This mosaic needs repair. It is based on one built at the Grand Central Terminal subway station in New York City in the early 1900s. Decide which of the new pieces here best match the originals. Cut them out and glue them to the damaged mosaic. This is how you would restore a real mosaic, using real stone, of course.

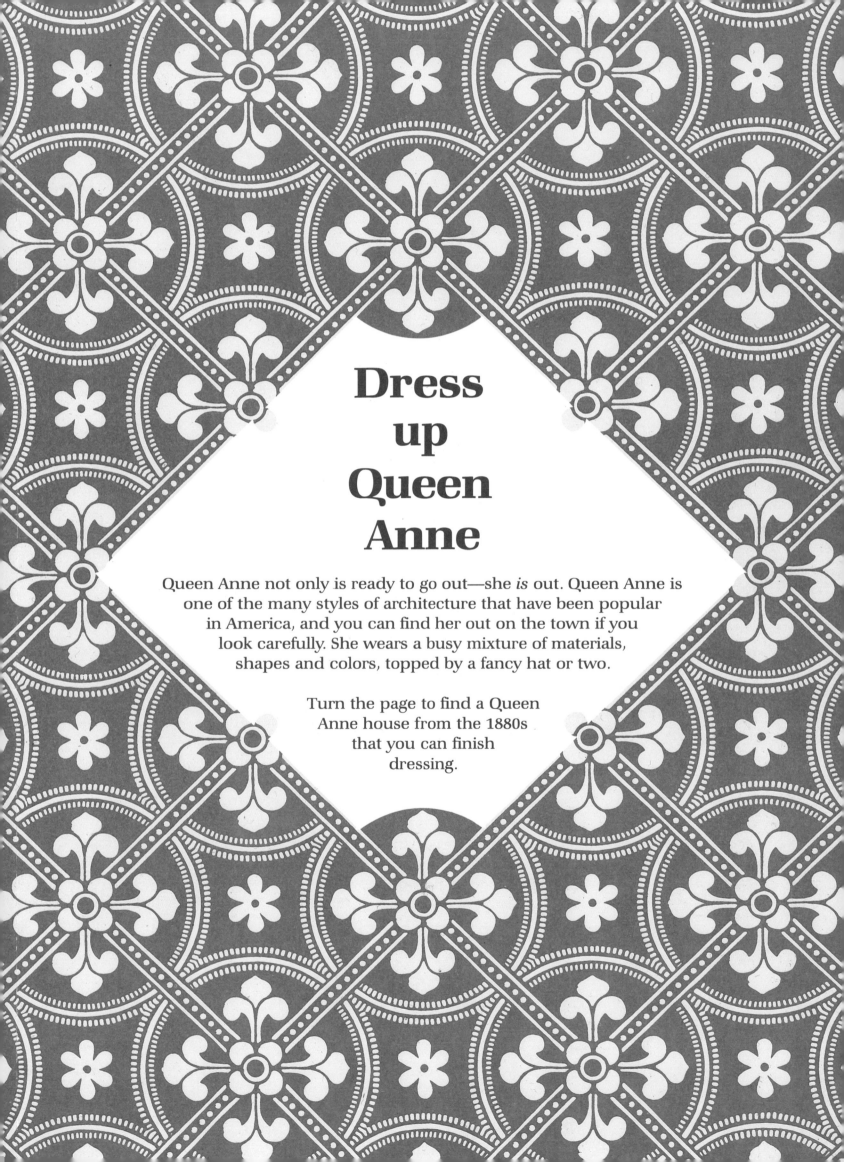

Dress up Queen Anne

Queen Anne not only is ready to go out—she *is* out. Queen Anne is one of the many styles of architecture that have been popular in America, and you can find her out on the town if you look carefully. She wears a busy mixture of materials, shapes and colors, topped by a fancy hat or two.

Turn the page to find a Queen Anne house from the 1880s that you can finish dressing.

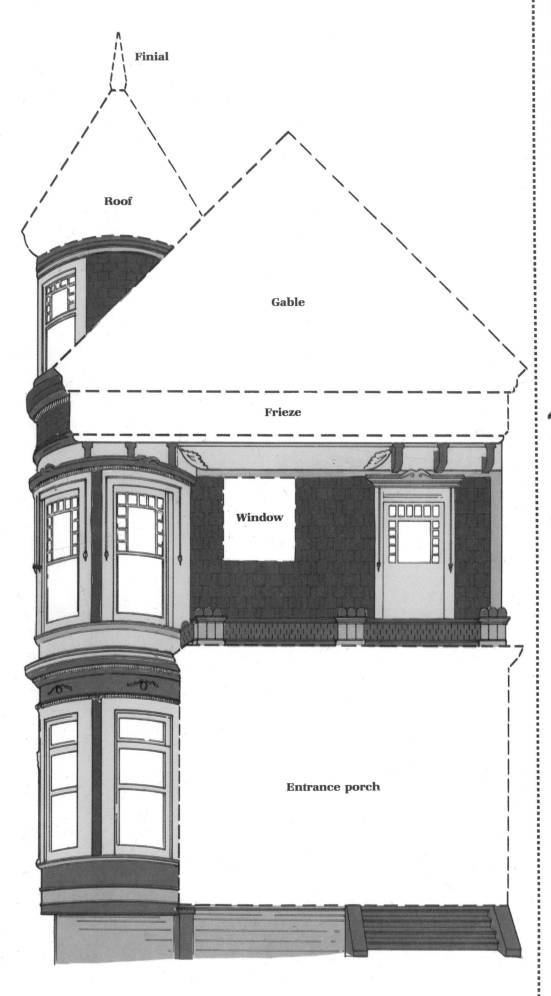

Finial

Roof

Gable

Frieze

Window

Entrance porch

To dress up this Queen Anne, you may want to cut along the dotted line to remove the house from the page. Then pick the parts that you think look best on her. Choose a porch, a new window, a gable for the front roof, a frieze below this, a roof for the tower and a finial to perch atop the roof. Cut out one or more parts and try them on. Glue the pieces you select onto the spaces with the dotted lines.

Finials

Roofs

Friezes

Gables

Windows

Entrance porches

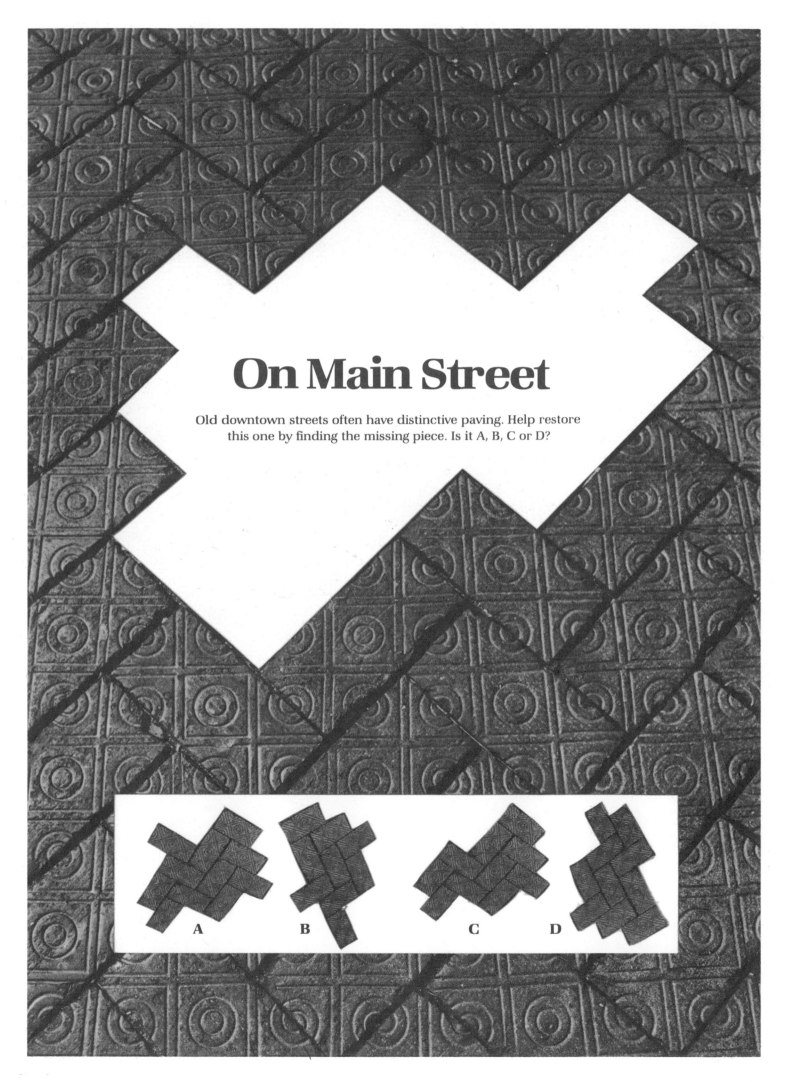

On Main Street

Old downtown streets often have distinctive paving. Help restore this one by finding the missing piece. Is it A, B, C or D?

A   B   C   D

1

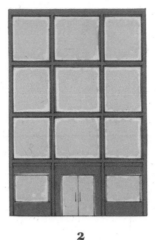

2

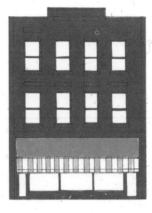

3

Bring back Main Street

Not too long ago, people who lived in small towns and cities all shopped in the same place: downtown on Main Street. Today, many people like to go to shopping malls, which often means that stores on Main Street lose business and close. When they do, the buildings may be abandoned or torn down. Because Main Streets have interesting buildings and because

stores there are still needed, preservationists all around the country are trying to restore them. They work with businesses and officials to fix up the stores, develop services that people want and bring residents and tourists back to shop, eat and visit.

You can help bring back Main Street. Pretend that you are a member of the town design review board. Your job is to make sure that new

buildings and preservation projects look right. On your old Main Street, a building burned down, so there is a gaping hole now. The store owner hired an architect to design a new building to fill in the space. The architect has sketched six proposals. Which of the six designs at the top best fits into the row? To find out, read the instructions at the right and fill in the chart.

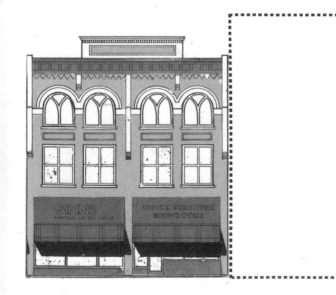

4

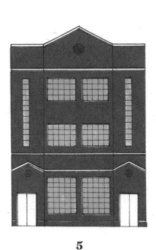

5

6

Cut out the two top parts above; tape them together. Do the same for the bottom parts. Also cut out the "infill" area in the dotted rectangle. Slide the top portion behind the bottom part, so you can see each building within the hole.

As you study each new building, fill out the chart. See how many elements of each design are the same as or similar to the existing Main Street buildings. Look at their:

Size and shape: Are they close to the same height? Taller? Shorter? Is the overall shape roughly similar?

Materials: Are the exterior materials, including the color, similar?

Roofs: Are the roof shapes and sizes like the older roofs?

Windows: Are the windows and panes of glass about the same size and shape as the originals?

Fill in "yes" or "no." Give your okay to the one with the most "yes" answers.

	1	2	3	4	5	6
Size and shape						
Materials						
Roofs						
Windows						

Star signs

If you travel through the Pennsylvania countryside where Pennsylvania Dutch settlers built farms, you will see many barns decorated with brightly colored designs. Most of these decorations are round and have geometric patterns such as the ones shown here. Flowers, animals and other artistic designs also were used.

These decorations once were called hex signs, because outsiders thought that they were intended to ward off harm and protect the crops and livestock. Actually, the barn signs are part of a folk tradition in which many items used every day—chairs, dishes, chests of drawers and doors—were painted with similar colorful designs.

How did the barn painters measure out the signs? They would make a compass using a pointer, a string or rope and a marker. The pointer with the string attached would be held firmly in place, and the painters would draw a circle radiating from the center point. You can try this yourself with a compass or a pin, string and a pencil. But first, "paint" your own barn sign using the pieces at right.

Adorn a door

Make a barn sign to hang on the door of your room. First, cut out the circle at right. Then cut out all the pieces below. Next, arrange the pieces on the circular pattern and glue them in place. If you like, punch two small holes near the top and knot a piece of string through each hole. Now your star sign is ready to hang.

Three of these houses are different from stencil number one. Can you find them?

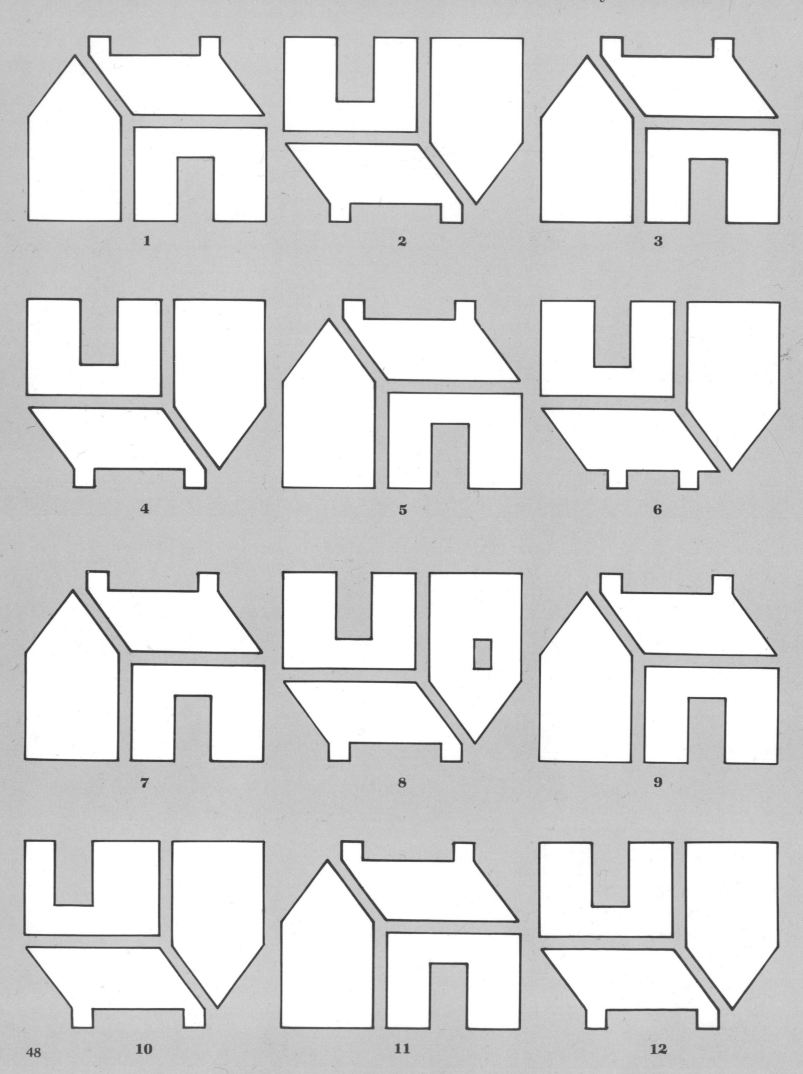

1

2

3

4

5

6

7

8

9

10

11

12

Welcome to stencil craft

In many early American homes, the walls, floors, furniture and curtains were decorated with stencil designs. Stenciling is the art of painting designs onto a surface using a cut-out paper pattern. The pattern is held tightly and covered with paint, using a stiff brush. The paint is applied only where the stencil has been cut, so the cut-out design is transferred onto the surface.

Sometimes the stenciling was done by the homeowner, sometimes by an itinerant (traveling) painter. These artists traveled from town to town and house to house to earn money by painting family portraits, wall murals, shop signs and stencils.

A wide variety of stencil designs were used. Many of them had specific meanings and were painted in particular rooms to convey a special message. Here are some popular designs:

Design	Meaning
House	Welcome
Pineapple	Hospitality
Weeping willow	Longevity
Thistle	Prosperity
Corn	Plenty

Directions

1. Cut the page on dotted line A.
2. Cut on dotted line B.
3. On the top piece, cut out the three yellow pieces of the stencil, being careful not to cut into the white background.
4. Place the stencil on top of the blank bottom piece. Secure it with masking or transparent tape folded over the top edges.
5. Using a watercolor marker or markers, color in the cut-out areas.
6. Remove the stencil carefully so you do not smear the design. Let it dry thoroughly.
7. You may hang your stencil design as a sign of welcome, glue it onto plain paper to use as a greeting card or think up other uses for it. You are welcome to use the stencil again.

A

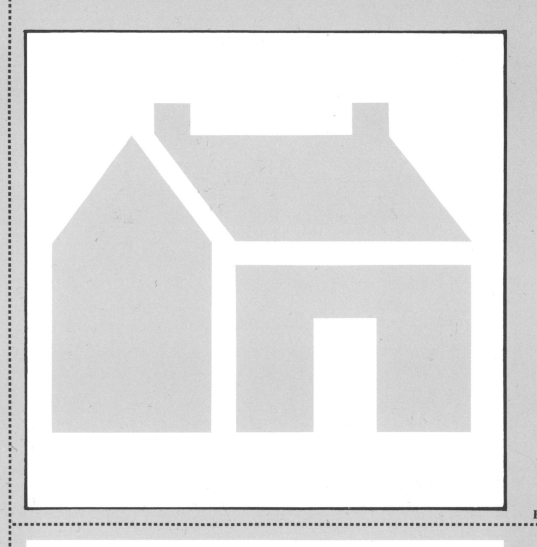

B

High atop the National Cathedral in Washington, D.C., sculptor Frederick Hart uses a pneumatic chisel to put the finishing touches on a reptilian gargoyle with a hammered lead downspout between its limestone fangs.

How to spot a gargoyle

If you look carefully at stone buildings along the street, you may see someone or something peering down at you. It may be a gargoyle. Gargoyles are decorative waterspouts carved from stone. Projecting from the top of or near the roof, they are attached to gutters to drain water away from a building, helping protect the structure from erosion.

During the Middle Ages in Europe between A.D. 500 and 1500, gargoyles were an important part of cathedral architecture. Stone carvers created scary-looking gargoyle creatures such as dragons and griffins, because they were thought to frighten away evil spirits and protect the cathedral and the people inside.

In the illustration above modern stone carvers work on gargoyles for the National Cathedral. For today's cathedrals gargoyles don't need to look scary. Some may be comic or just plain ordinary; some may commemorate a person or event; and some may represent a period of history or part of our popular culture.

You can draw your own special gargoyle in the blank space above. Then turn the page to make some gargoyle masks.

Gruesome gargoyle masks

Here are two pictures of carved gargoyles. Cut them out and insert string through the two small black circles on either side of each face, and you will have two scary masks to wear. These pictures would have frightened a child living in A.D. 1400. How about you?

The large gargoyle mask on this page is based on the caveman on the left at the National Cathedral. It was the last of the 106 gargoyles carved for the cathedral and sits on top of the north tower.

Many of the cathedral's gargoyles tell stories or jokes. What story do you think is behind the carving on the right of a woman with a camera?

The mask on this page is based on a stone carving that originally graced a building in Chicago.

To the left and right are two animal gargoyles from the National Cathedral: an elephant and a man catching a pig. What stories could be behind these?

Wooden wonders

How would you cross a river? Before we had breathtaking big bridges, you might have used a log or a simple bed of stones or, in Roman times, an arched span. Or, you might have been ferried across in a boat.

In the early days of the United States, logs and planks were often used as temporary bridges. But many of them rotted away or collapsed.

Better bridges were needed to improve the country's transportation system. Early in the 19th century bridge builders developed trusses to support stronger bridges. Trusses often look like lattice made up of many triangles and can be built from metal or wood. Ones made of wood, however, do not survive rain and snow for long. So a solution was thought of: roofs to cover the trusses.

And that's why a covered bridge is covered—to protect the bridge itself, not the people who use it!

Thousands of covered bridges were built in America (although the idea came from Europe) until more efficient metal bridges were developed. Not many covered bridges are left, but here is one you can construct yourself.

Directions

1. Cut out parts A (floor and walls), B and C (ends), D (roof), E and F (road) and G, H, I and J (stone walls). Make sure you cut along the dotted lines on part D.
2. Fold the two walls up on part A with the vertical boards outside and the trusses inside. Fold tabs in.
3. Fold and glue the tabs of B and C inside the ends of part A.
4. Crease the roof down the center; fold and glue the ends inside. Center the roof on part A and glue or tape the tabs of part A to the inside of the roof, making the roof's edges cover the tabs.
5. On parts E and F fold the tabs down and tape or glue tabs 1 and 2 to 3 and 4 to create a boxlike end.
6. Take parts G, H, I and J and line up the point of grass with the low end of each side of the road. Glue the walls onto the road's bent tabs. The bridge rests on the high end of each of the roads.
7. Cut out the rocky stream and place it under the bridge. You can fold up part of the stream's rocky bank to give it a more three-dimensional effect. Cut out the man and horse and glue or tape it so it stands up.

Now enjoy the view!

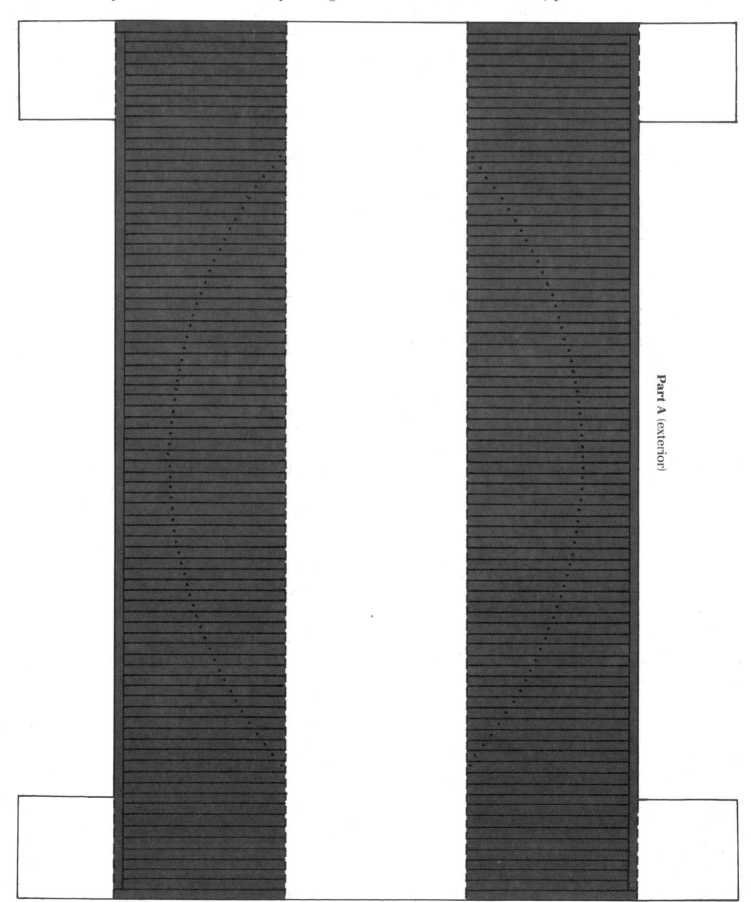

Part A (exterior)

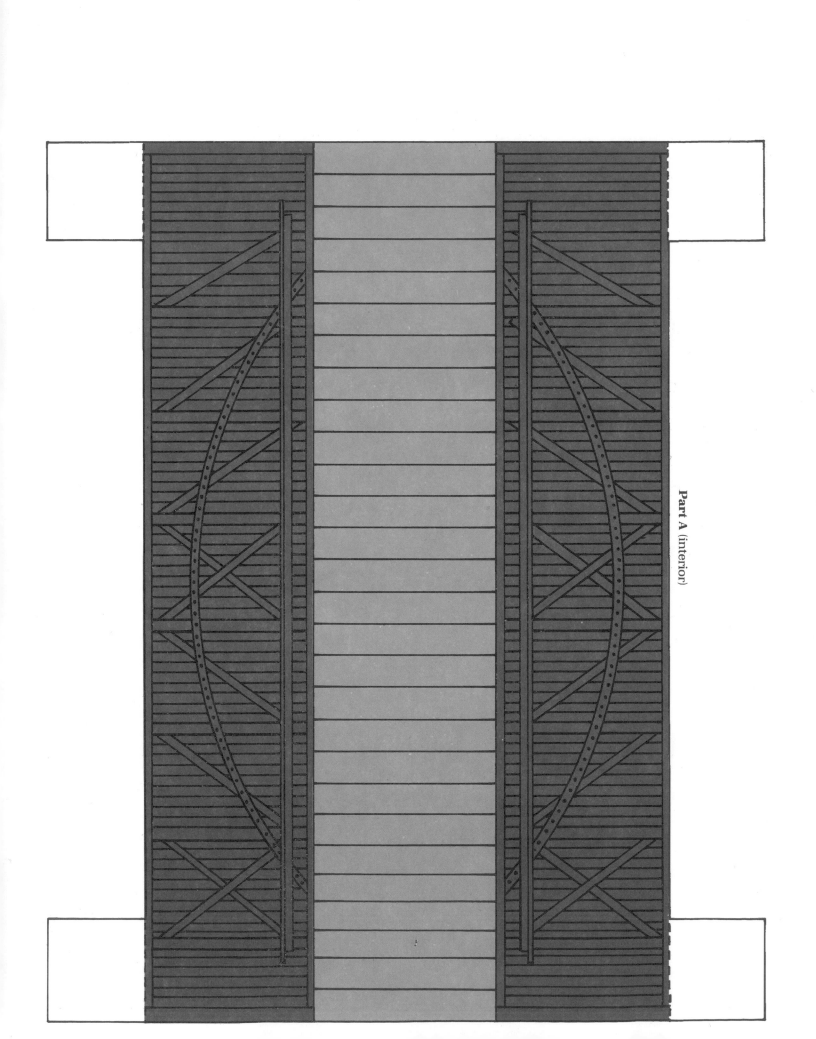

Part A (interior)

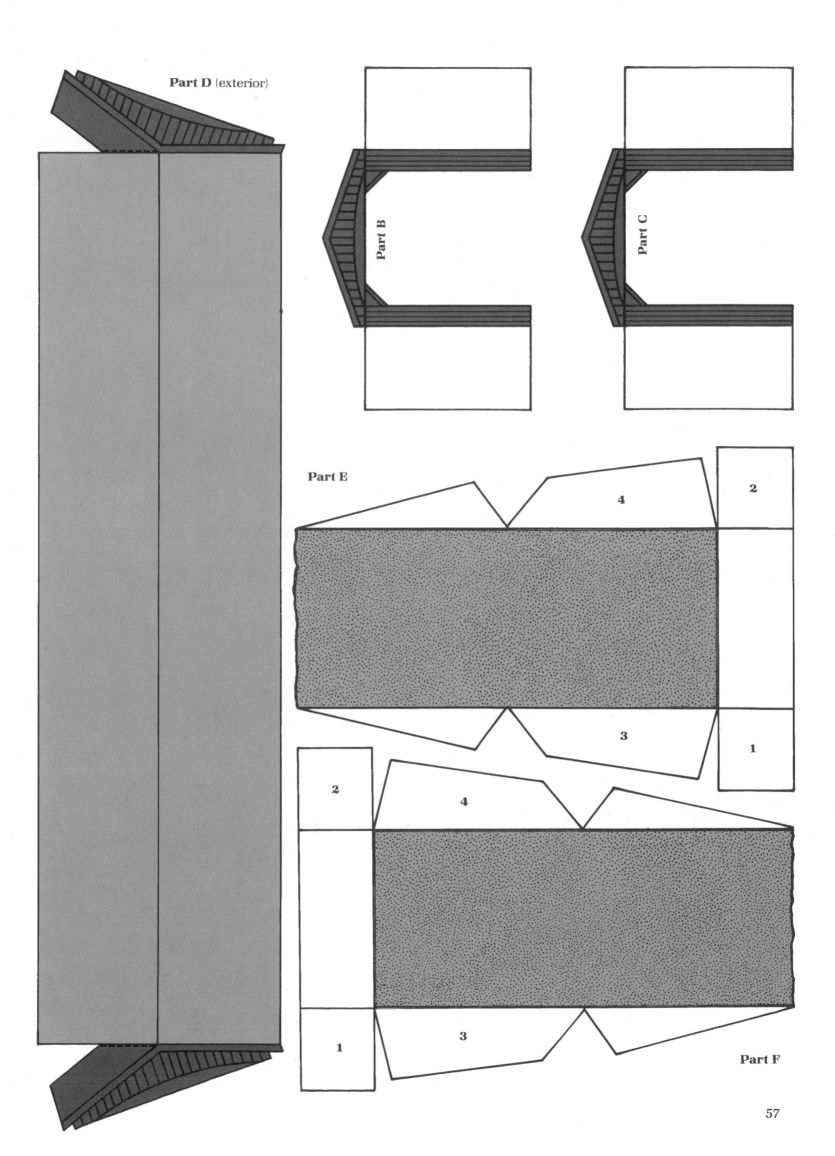

Part D (exterior)

Part B

Part C

Part E

2

4

3

1

2

4

3

1

Part F

57

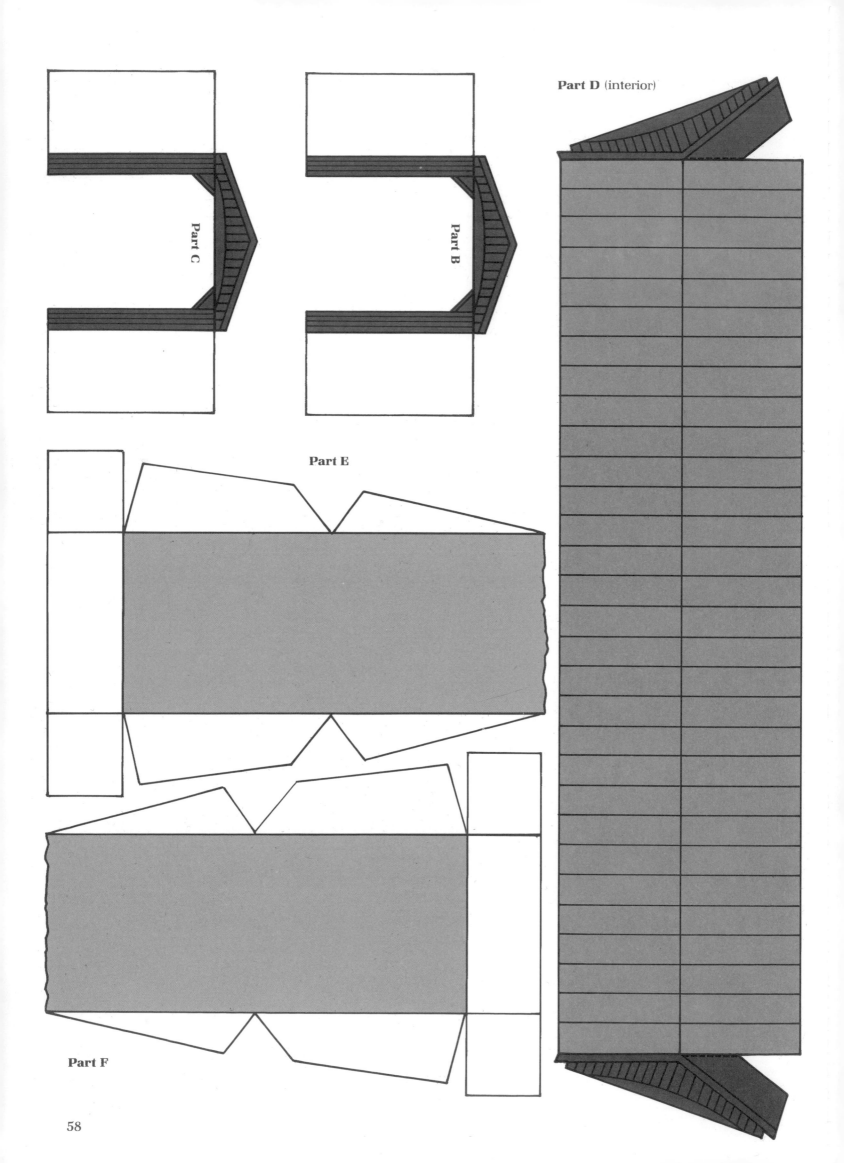

Part C

Part B

Part D (interior)

Part E

Part F

Part G   Part H   Part I   Part J

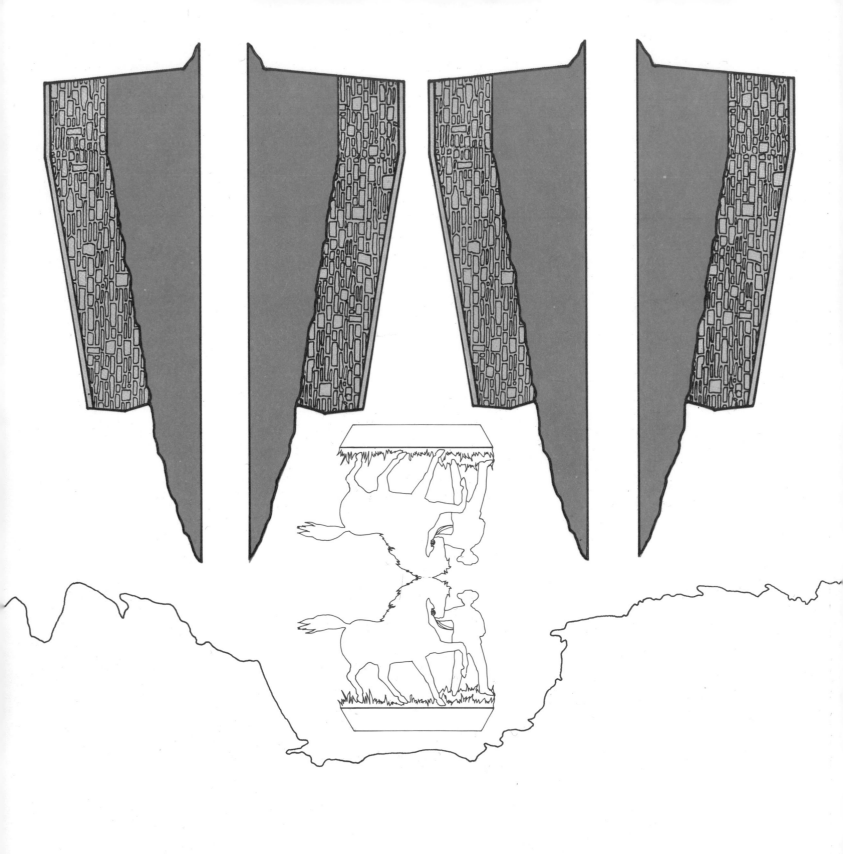

Go build!

Match architects with their buildings

Read the directions on the following pages and then cut out all 44 cards.

Robert Mills (1781–1855)
Fireproof Building
Treasury Building
Washington Monument

Frederick Law Olmsted (1822–1903)
Central Park
Town Plan, Riverside, Ill.
Stanford University Plan

Louis H. Sullivan (1856–1924)
Auditorium Building
Merchants' National Bank
Wainwright Building

Charles Follen McKim (1847–1909)
William Rutherford Mead (1846–1928)
Stanford White (1853–1906)
Boston Public Library
Pennsylvania Station
Villard Houses

Ludwig Mies van der Rohe (1886–1969)
Crown Hall, Ill. Institute of Technology
Farnsworth House
Lake Shore Drive Apartments

Thomas Jefferson (1743–1826)
Monticello
University of Virginia
Virginia State Capitol

Julia Morgan (1872–1957)
First Church of Christ, Scientist
Hearst Castle
Turner Stores

Benjamin Henry Latrobe (1764–1820)
Decatur House
St. John's Church
U.S. Capitol

Charles Bulfinch (1763–1844)
India Wharf
Massachusetts General Hospital
Massachusetts State House

Henry Hobson Richardson (1838–86)
Allegheny County Courthouse and Jail
J. J. Glessner House
Trinity Church

Frank Lloyd Wright (1867–1959)
Frederick C. Robie House
Johnson Wax Building
Solomon R. Guggenheim Museum

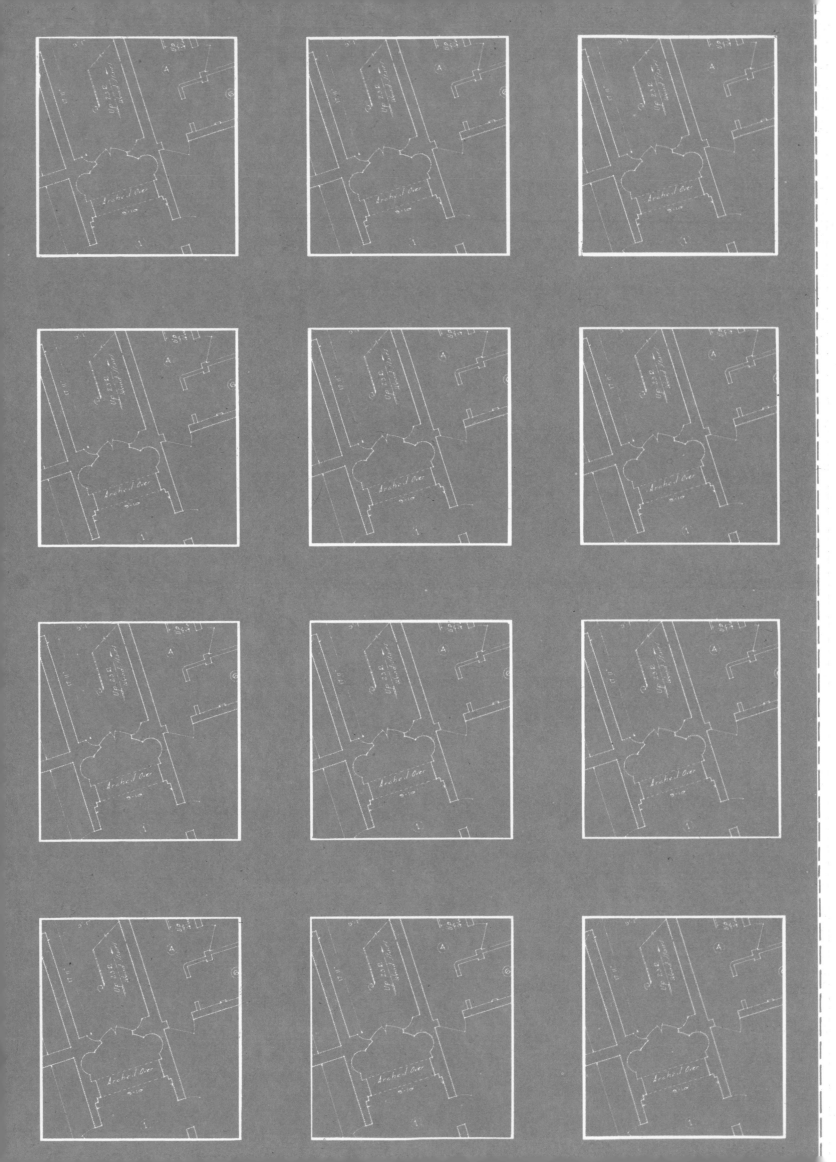

The object of **Go build!** is to match each architect with three buildings the architect has designed. The game contains 11 sets of 4 cards each—1 architect card and 3 building cards. Two to six persons may play.

1. Shuffle the deck and deal 7 cards (for two players) or 5 cards (more than two players). Place the remaining cards face down as stock.

continued

Johnson Wax Building
Frank Lloyd Wright
1936, 1944
Racine, Wis.

Town Plan
Frederick Law Olmsted
1869
Riverside, Ill.

Virginia State Capitol
Thomas Jefferson
1785–98
Richmond, Va.

Central Park
Frederick Law Olmsted
1858–80
New York, N.Y.

Allegheny County Courthouse and Jail
Henry Hobson Richardson
1883–88
Pittsburgh, Pa.

Frederick C. Robie House
Frank Lloyd Wright
1909
Chicago, Ill

Decatur House
Benjamin Henry Latrobe
1818–19
Washington, D.C.

Pennsylvania Station
McKim, Mead and White
1902–10; demolished
New York, N.Y.

Massachusetts State House
Charles Bulfinch
1795–97
Boston, Mass.

Wainwright Building
Louis H. Sullivan with Dankmar Adler
1886–90
St. Louis, Mo.

Fireproof Building
Robert Mills
1821
Charleston, S.C.

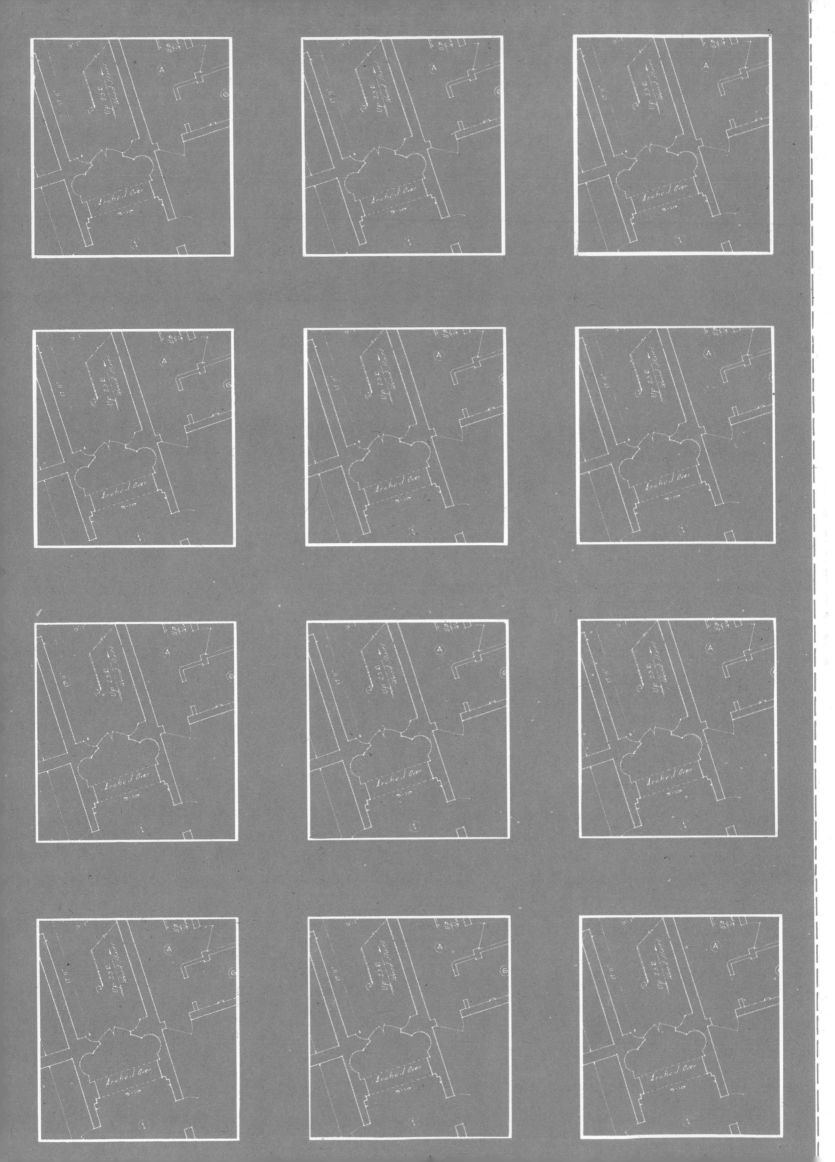

2. The player on the dealer's left begins the game by asking another player for either building cards of a specific architect ("Give me your Bulfinches") or an architect face card ("Give me Bulfinch"). The player addressed must give up all building cards by the architect named or the face card. If the player has none of the cards requested, he or she replies, "Go build!" Then the

continued

J. J. Glessner House
Henry Hobson Richardson
1885–87
Chicago, Ill.

Stanford University Plan
Frederick Law Olmsted
1887–91
Palo Alto, Calif.

St. John's Church
Benjamin Henry Latrobe
1816
Washington, D.C.

Solomon R. Guggenheim Museum
Frank Lloyd Wright
1943–59
New York, N.Y.

Villard Houses
McKim, Mead and White
1882–85
New York, N.Y.

Monticello
Thomas Jefferson
1768–1809
Charlottesville, Va.

Crown Hall, Illinois Institute of Technology
Ludwig Mies van der Rohe
1950–56
Chicago, Ill.

Auditorium Building
Louis H. Sullivan with Dankmar Adler
1886–90
Chicago, Ill.

Corncob Capital, U.S. Capitol
Benjamin Henry Latrobe
1806
Washington, D.C.

Boston Public Library
McKim, Mead and White
1887–95
Boston, Mass.

Lake Shore Drive Apartments
Ludwig Mies van der Rohe
1948–51
Chicago, Ill.

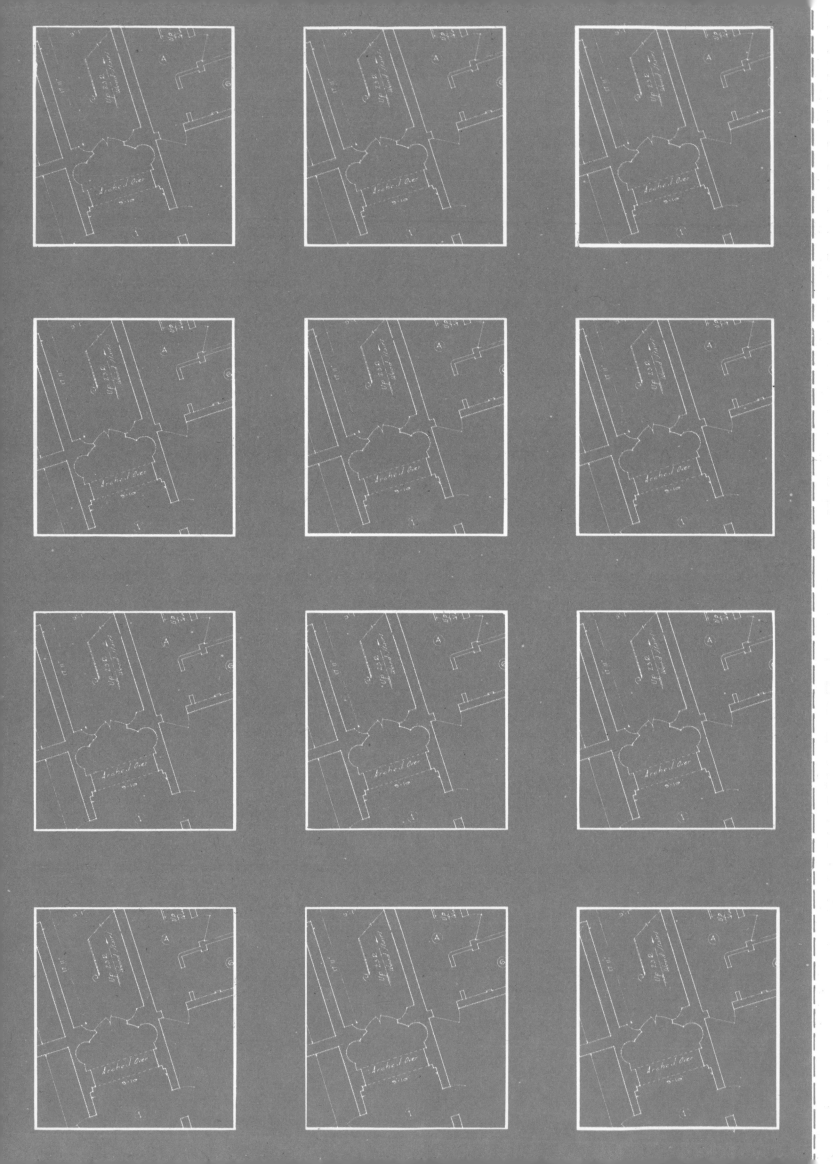

asker takes a card from the stock.

3. A player's turn continues as long as he or she receives or selects from stock the requested cards. Then the turn passes to the player on the left. As sets are made, place them face up. When all cards have been gathered into sets, the game ends. The player with the most sets wins the game.

Now, go build!

Hearst Castle
Julia Morgan
1919–39
San Simeon, Calif.

Massachusetts General Hospital
Charles Bulfinch
1818–23
Boston, Mass.

India Wharf
Charles Bulfinch
1803–07
Boston, Mass.

Farnsworth House
Ludwig Mies van der Rohe
1945–50
Plano, Ill.

University of Virginia
Thomas Jefferson
1817–26
Charlottesville, Va.

Turner Stores
Julia Morgan
1942
Berkeley, Calif.

Treasury Building
Robert Mills
1836–69
Washington, D.C.

Merchants' National Bank
Louis H. Sullivan
1914
Grinnell, Iowa

Trinity Church
Henry Hobson Richardson
1872–77
Boston, Mass.

Washington Monument
Robert Mills
1848–84
Washington, D.C.

First Church of Christ, Scientist
Julia Morgan
1910
Berkeley, Calif.

Going to school in 1862

You probably don't go to school in a one-room schoolhouse, because few of them are left. But for 250 years, until the early 1900s, most American children—perhaps even some of your relatives—went to small country schools such as the one in the diorama here for you to build and furnish.

What did these schools look like? Everybody talks about the "little red schoolhouse," but most of them were not red. Wooden ones might be painted white. Other schools were made of stone, brick and logs. Some were square, some rectangular, others octagonal.

Inside nearly every school had a potbellied stove for heat and maybe a blackboard, shelves and a cloakroom for coats. Furniture could be rough and uncomfortable, with several students sharing a desk. Boys and girls often sat on opposite sides of the room.

At the front was the teacher, who taught students of all ages their 3Rs—readin', 'ritin' and 'rithmetic—plus some history, geography and music if time allowed. Older students helped teach the younger ones.

These schools, with their recitals, spelling bees and celebrations, were the center of community life. A lot was learned in just one room.

Directions

1. Cut out the wall and floor piece. Fold up the wall. Fold in tabs A, B, C, D and E.
2. Cut out the front end [1]. Fold in tabs F and G. Tape the end to tabs A and B.
3. Cut out the back end [2]. Fold in tabs H and I. Tape the end to tabs D and E.
4. Cut out the roof. Fold on the dotted line. Tape the full side to tab C. Tape tabs G and H to the full side of the roof. Tape tabs F and I to the short side of the roof.
5. Cut out the bell tower. Fold it into a box and tape it closed. Fold tab J. Fold tab K twice. Tape tab J to tab K. Fold in tabs L and M. Tape the bell tower to box 1 on the roof.
6. Cut out the chimney. Fold it into a box and tape it closed. Fold in tabs N and O. Tape the chimney to box 2 on the roof.
7. Cut out the other figures to furnish the inside and outside of the school. Move them around as you like.

Note: To make the diorama as strong as possible, you may glue the tabs and then tape over them with transparent tape.

1

2

The country school that served as a model for your diorama is a real schoolhouse still standing in Norwalk, Conn. Named the Broad River Community Schoolhouse, this little building opened its doors in 1862. The teacher was George L. Finney, and he was paid $20 a month. For the next 62 years, school was held here, with as many as 48 students each term.

The school is 22 by 44 feet in size and has wood siding on its outside walls. It is a simple version of the Italianate style. Plans for the school were prepared by Eli K. Street, a carpenter. He was paid $5 for the plans and completed the school in late 1861. The lot and construction costs together totaled a little more than $700.

When a new town school was built in 1924, the old schoolhouse was turned into a community center and meeting place. In 1980 the building was sold to a company that was very interested in restoring it for a new use. Some people turn old schools into homes, stores or museums. But this company had another good idea: a branch bank.

The Fairfield County Savings Bank researched how the schoolhouse looked originally and hired architect Richard Bergmann to adapt it for its new use. One thing he found out was that the school was never red, or even white. It was a light brown color with green trim and shutters, popular Victorian colors.

On the bank's opening day, one of the first customers was a former student at the Broad River Schoolhouse.

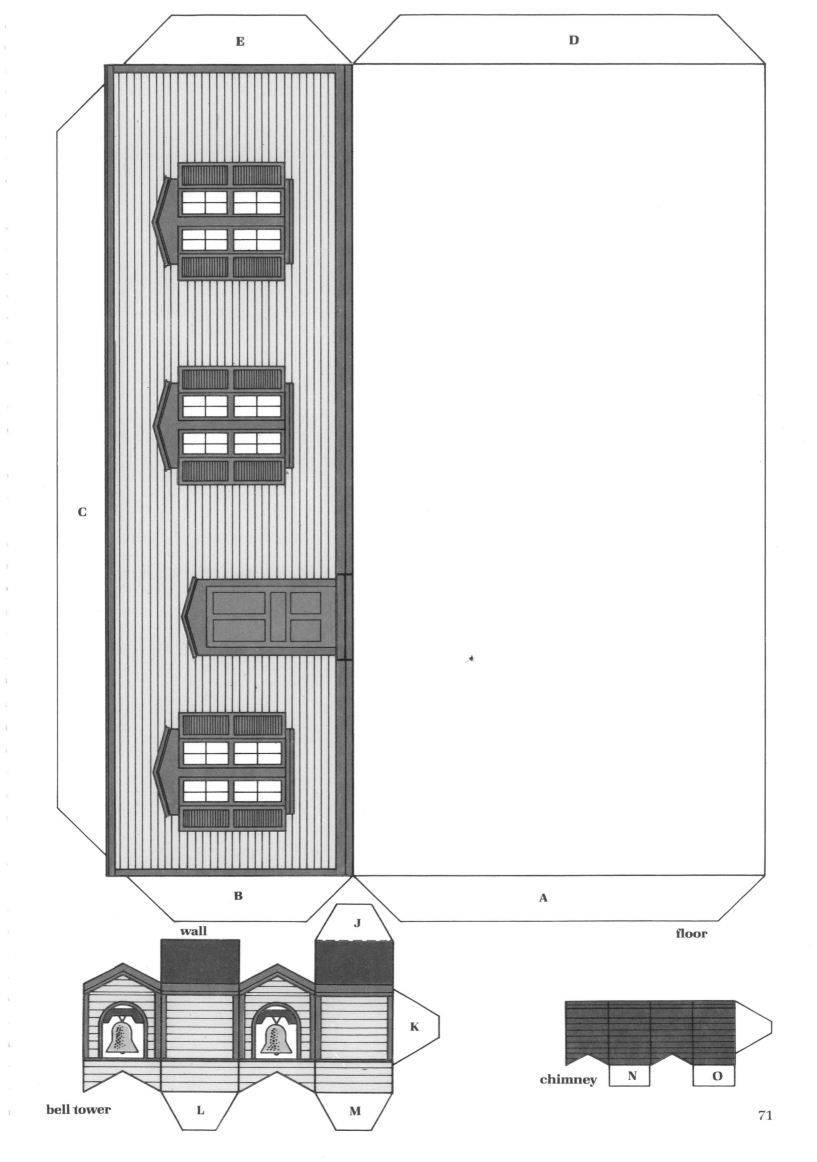

E

D

C

L

B

wall

J

K

A

floor

bell tower

L

M

chimney

N

O

71

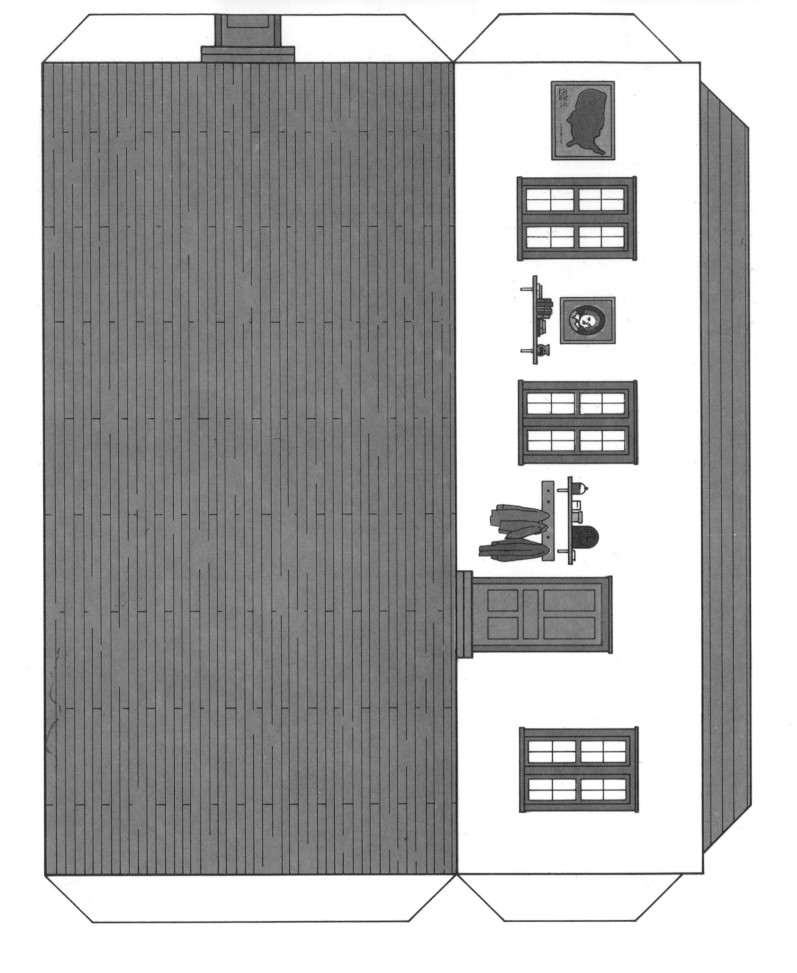

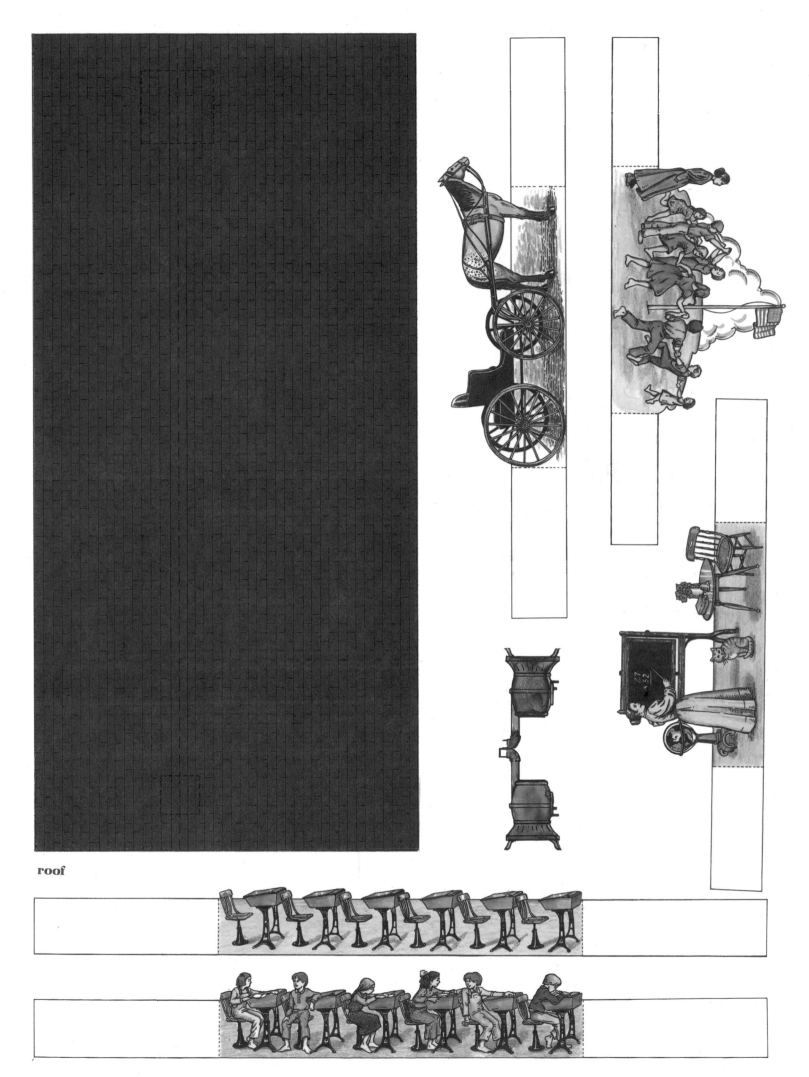

roof

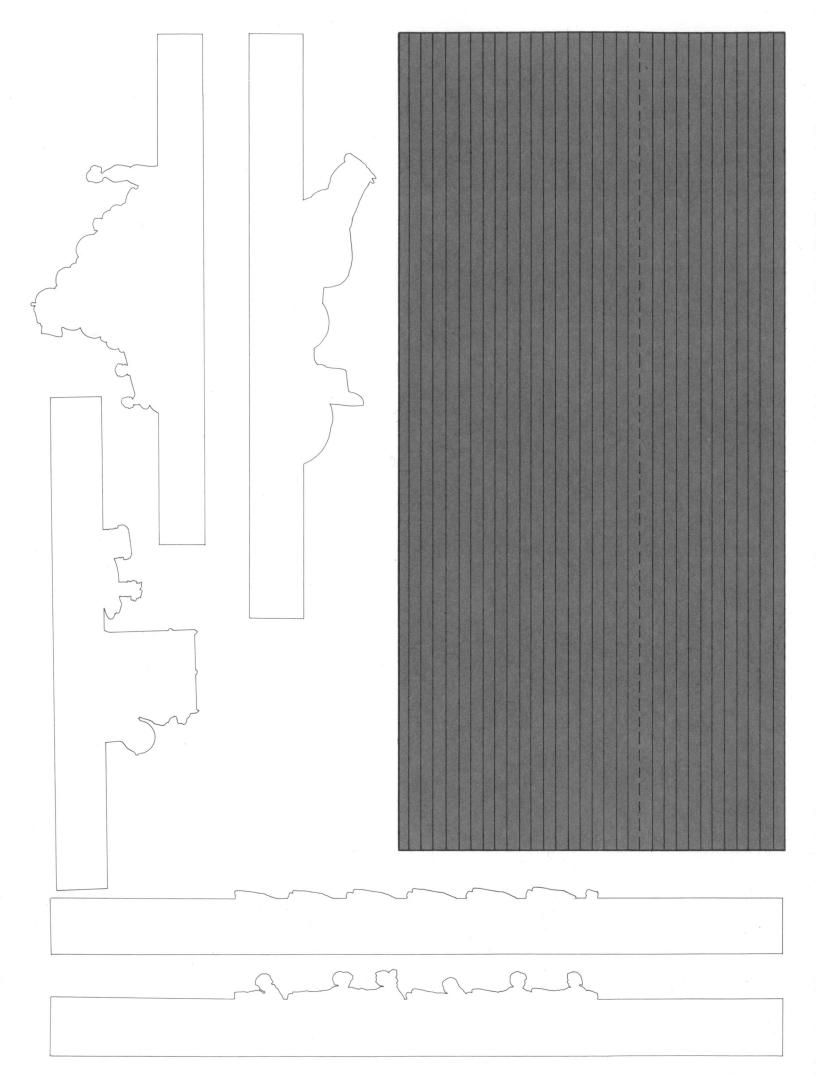

Light work

Here are five famous American lighthouses. All were built to help ships navigate by directing them away from the shore. Put together five correct lighthouse puzzles with six pieces each by cutting out all the pieces and rearranging them into sets. Use the illustrations at left as a guide.

Cape Hatteras Lighthouse (1870), N.C. The tallest brick light tower in America, this lighthouse on the dangerous Outer Banks of North Carolina has saved many ships from the Graveyard of the Atlantic. Because the sea is moving in, the lighthouse may be relocated to save it.

Old Point Loma Lighthouse (1855), San Diego, Calif. Although not as tall as other lighthouses, this one was located on a high cliff 462 feet above the sea—so high that it was often lost in the clouds. Because of this, it was replaced in 1891 by a light closer to sea level.

Fowey Rocks Lighthouse (1878), Cape Florida, Fla. Located southeast of Key Biscayne, this hexagonal steel framework was an engineering marvel of its day. It was needed to keep ships from crashing on the reefs, but one even wrecked while the lighthouse was being built.

Spectacle Reef Light (1874), Mich. Built to keep ships off another treacherous reef, the light at Spectacle Reef helped guide sailors toward the Straits of Mackinac and into Lake Michigan. It was constructed on a difficult, cold site and took four years to complete.

West Quoddy Head Light (1808), Maine. This is the northernmost of nearly 70 lighthouses in Maine, which is often called the Lighthouse State. With its red and white stripes, the light tower looks like a big candy cane. It had one of the first fog bells installed in the United States.

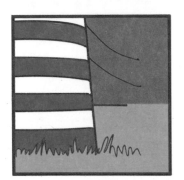

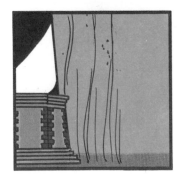

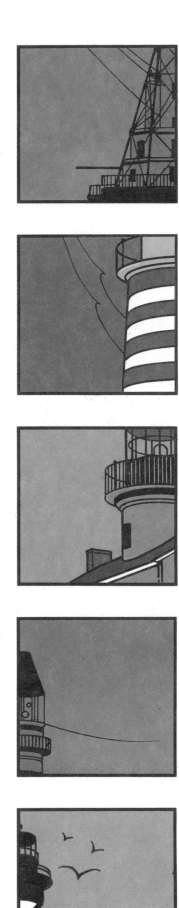

Being a fireman in the early days of the nation was a lot like being a member of a club. Until the middle of the 1800s most fire companies were made up of volunteers rather than the paid firefighters we have today. Although they risked their lives to keep their towns safe from fire, early firemen enjoyed their work because it was a special honor.

One thing that set the firemen apart was their uniforms. Many had a set for work and another for ceremonies. The felt top hats shown here looked good in parades, decorated with fire company symbols. (More are on page 83.) For show, firemen also wore colorful short capes. For work, their typical uniform was a double-breasted red shirt and black pants with boots. Later, a helmet like firefighters now wear became popular. Today's uniforms are much lighter and more practical—but they are not quite as much fun.

Who'll save old No. 9?

Fire stations used to be called names like Vigilant, Perseverance, Relief and Hope. Now they are more likely to be named Engine Company No. 1 or Truck Company No. 9. But whatever they are known as, fire stations have been important buildings in American towns for a long time.

They started out as little more than sheds in which to store engines, buckets, hooks and ladders. When a fire started and the alarm rang, all the people in town were expected to come help put out the fire.

In the 1700s the first fire companies were formed. Members were private citizens who volunteered particularly to help save their own property. Later they offered to fight fires throughout a town. Benjamin Franklin and George Washington were members of such companies, which sometimes were housed in existing public buildings.

By the early 1800s volunteer fire companies started to spring up. Similar to social clubs, they were important enough that towns began to build special buildings just for the fire companies. The equipment was stored downstairs, below the meeting rooms. The buildings were simple but solid looking, and many were in the Greek Revival style with a pointed roof. Tall towers for drying fire hoses were introduced in the 1840s, followed by large garage doors for larger engines.

When towns decided in the mid-19th century to turn their volunteer fire companies into paid, professional ones, the design of fire houses also changed. They began to look more important, with fancy decoration in all the popular architectural styles. More room was needed downstairs for the horses that now drew the engines. Upstairs was where the firemen slept. Soon, devices were added to help the firemen reach fires more quickly, including a sliding pole to the ground floor.

The work that fire stations perform, and the people and equipment they house, explain why fire stations look the way they do.

Fire chief   **Historian**   **Student**   **Neighbor**

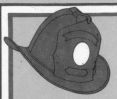

How to play "Who'll save old No. 9?"

Preparation:

1. Carefully cut out the four markers below (the neighbor, the student, the historian and the fire chief).
2. Fold the markers in half and tape or glue the sides together. Fold the half circles out and tape each marker to a penny.
3. Carefully tear out the game board on the dotted lines and tape the two halves together.
4. Cut out the 16 Fire Alarm Cards and place them on the board.
5. Borrow a die from another game.

Rules of the game:

The game is best with four players, but two or three persons may play.

1. Choose a marker.
2. Roll the die. The person who rolls the highest number goes first. The game then continues clockwise.
3. On your turn, move the number of spaces indicated on the die. Follow any instructions on the square you land on.
4. If you land on a Fire Alarm Card square, take the top card in the pile and follow the card's instructions. Fire Alarm Cards marked "Save this card for an emergency" can be saved and used later if you land on a square telling you to move back. These cards permit you to stay in place. All Fire Alarm Cards should be returned to the bottom of the pile after use.
5. You may take advantage of a Bonus square only if the square is marked with your own player (for instance, the student player must land on the Student Bonus square).
6. To take the short cut, you must land exactly on the Short Cut circle. Otherwise your move continues down the board and you skip the Short Cut circle.
7. To win, you must land exactly in the fire station. If you roll too high a number, you must wait until your next turn to roll again and try to get the exact number.

Get fired up!

Many old fire stations are still around, still serving the same fire companies that they always have. But in other places, old firehouses no longer serve modern firefighting needs and are being closed down.

On the next pages, you will find a game about one old firehouse—old No. 9. It was built around 1885 and is a warm, red brick—just right for a firehouse. Decorations include interesting stonework, a tower with a weathervane and a balcony.

The city government has announced that this fire station, located in midtown, is going to be closed. It is too small for the big new fire trucks and new equipment. A larger fire station serving the whole town will be built on a larger site. The mayor has not said what will happen to the old firehouse, but rumors are that it is about to be sold.

Can old No. 9 be saved? How? Your job, as you play the game, is to get fired up enough to save it.

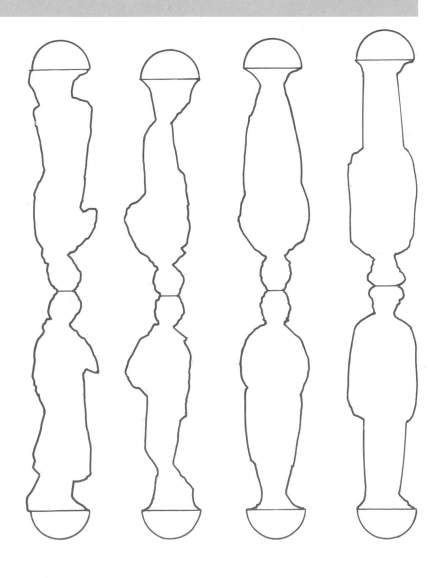

Developer wants
to save only the
firehouse facade
and build a highrise
behind it
Go back 3

Businesses donate
money for campaign

Go ahead 2

Save this card
for an emergency!

*You don't
have to move back*

Fire chiefs
association
urges preservation

Go ahead 1

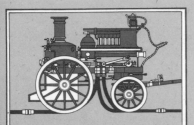

Save this card
for an emergency!

*You don't
have to move back*

Rain
cancels rally

Roll again

Fire! magazine
publishes
a story

Go ahead 1

Governor
takes an interest
in the firehouse

Roll again

Station kitchen
catches on fire

Go back 3

New firehouse
may not be built

Go ahead 2

Save this card
for an emergency!

*You don't
have to move back*

City holiday.
No work today

Roll again

Save this card
for an emergency!

*You don't
have to move back*

History
of firehouse
published

Go ahead 1

Firehouse dog
Dalmation Dan
goes on TV

Go ahead 1

Save this card
for an emergency!

*You don't
have to move back*

The Hibernia Engine Company No. 1 was established in Philadelphia in 1752. Its members were all Irish, which is why it was called Hibernia (another name for Ireland). This illustration shows the firehouse in 1857 with its members preparing to leave for a parade. They wore green dress capes decorated with the company's emblem, an eagle on a harp (for Ireland). The mascot rests in front of a fancy engine with painted panels. The firemen have silver trumpets and axes. Notice that the building, with a wide ground-floor door for the engine and smaller rooms on the upper stories, looks more important than the buildings around it.

Who'll save old No. 9?

START →

Roll again · FOR SALE SIGN APPEARS · Go ahead 1 · DEVELOPER OFFERS TO BUY FIREHOUSE · Go ahead 4 · STUDENT BONUS · Go ahead 1 · HISTORIAN RESEARCHES FIREHOUSE HISTORY · Go ahead 3 · NEIGHBORS FORM A PRESERVATION GROUP

DEVELOPER WANTS TO TEAR IT DOWN · Go back 1

PRESERVATION GROUP APPEALS TO MAYOR · Go ahead 1

FIRE ALARM CARD · Choose one from the stack

PRESERVATIONISTS GO BEFORE CITY COUNCIL · Go ahead 2

NEIGHBOR BONUS · Go ahead 4

FIRE ALARM CARD · Choose one from the stack

JUDGE STOPS DEMOLITION · Go ahead 3

FAMOUS ARCHITECT URGES PRESERVATION · Go ahead 1

STUDENT BONUS · Go ahead 4

DEVELOPER SELLS FIREHOUSE · Go ahead 1

FIRE ALARM CARD · Choose one from the stack

RESTAURANT OFFERS TO BUY FIREHOUSE · Go ahead 1

HISTORIAN BONUS · Go ahead 4

SALE COMPLETED · Go ahead 3

FIRE ALARM CARD · Choose one from the stack

HOT CHILI CAFE PROPOSED · Go ahead 2

FIRE CHIEF BONUS · Go ahead 4

FIRE ALARM CARD · Choose one from the stack

BALCONY COLLAPSES · Go back 2

NEIGHBOR BONUS · Go ahead 4

FIRE ALARM CARD · Choose one from the stack

BUILDING PASSES HEALTH INSPECTION · Go ahead 1

FIRE ALARM CARD · Choose one from the stack

STORY APPEARS ON NETWORK NEWS · Go ahead 2

DALMATION DAN'S CHILI CAFE OPENS · Roll again

NO. 9

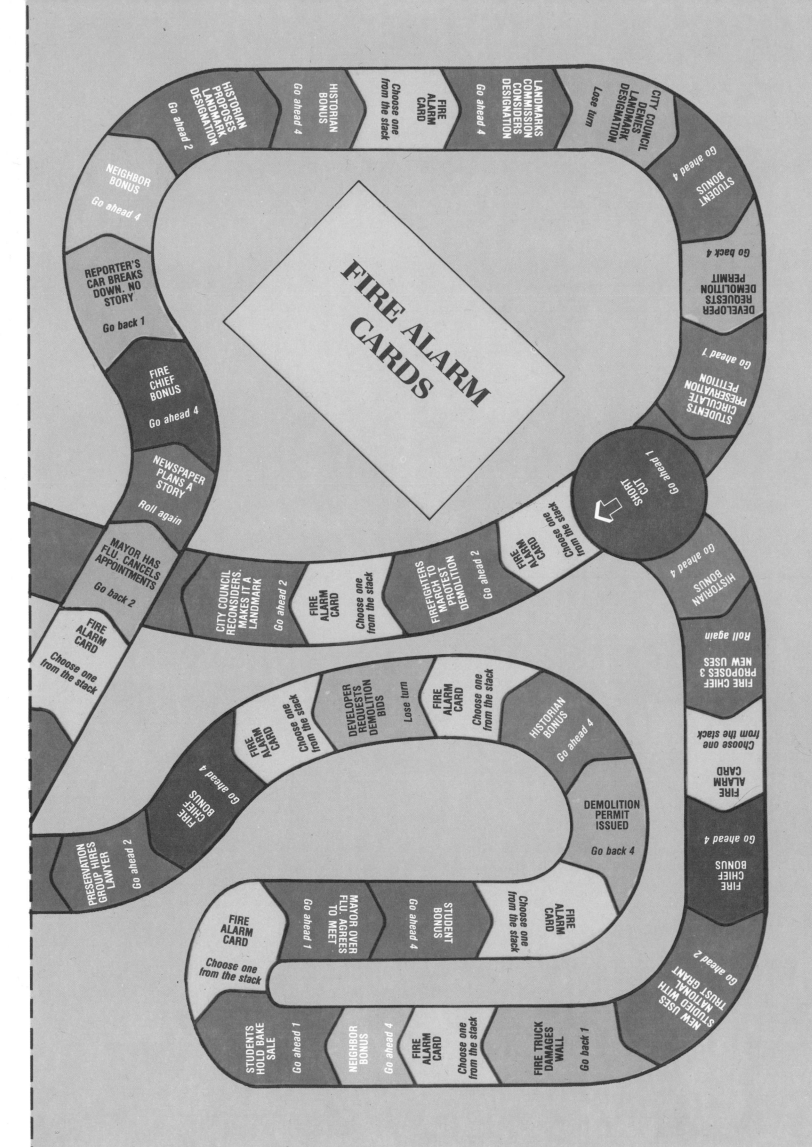

Archi-venture
A treasure hunt

The pictures below also appear elsewhere in this book. Can you find the page on which each picture is, or was, located and write the page number (or the activity) on the correct line below?

This treasure hunt should give you an adventure in architecture—you could call it an archi-venture.

1

2

3

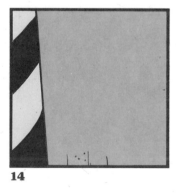
4

5

6

7

8

9

10

11

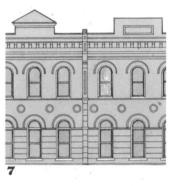
12

13

14

15

16

1. _____

2. _____

3. _____

4. _____

5. _____

6. _____

7. _____

8. _____

9. _____

10. _____

11. _____

12. _____

13. _____

14. _____

15. _____

16. _____

Credits

Building with nature   With thanks to the Utah Heritage Foundation's *Architecture Is Elementary* by Nathan B. Winters (Peregrine Smith, 1986). p. 4, photographs, all Wendy Cortesi. p. 5, nos. 1 and 5, Balthazar Korab; 2 and 6, Wendy Cortesi; 3, © 1982 Van Bucher, Photo Researchers; 4, Robert A. Baird, Historical Arts and Casting; 7 and 8, NTHP; 9, James Chotas.

Who settled where?   Drawings, Historic American Buildings Survey, National Park Service; photograph, Ukrainian Museum, New York City.

Voices from the past   Drawings, HABS.

History mystery   p. 10–12, drawings, Richard Schlecht. p. 13, photograph and poster, U.S. Borax and Chemical Corporation.

How houses change   Drawings, Roz Schanzer.

Picture this   The Quilt Digest Press, San Francisco.

A-mazing landmarks   Plan of Washington, D.C., Library of Congress; map and drawings, Elsie Hennig.

Block by block   With thanks to Richard Bierce, AIA. Drawings, HABS.

Down on the farm   Painting, Josyln Art Museum, Omaha. Drawings, Wendy Cortesi.

Watch out for ducks!   p. 22, all, © John Margolies, ESTO. p. 23, all color, © John Margolies, ESTO; duck moving, Martha Cooper/*People Weekly* © 1988 Time Inc.

What does your garden say?   Drawing from and garden outline based on drawing in *American Gardens of the 19th Century* by Ann Leighton (University of Massachusetts Press, 1987). Nos. 1, 2, 3, 5, 7 and 8, Harper Horticultural Slide Library; 4 and 6, Wendy Cortesi.

An architectural rebus   Drawings, Loel Barr.

I'm sign smart   Horse, hammer and ice cream cone, © John Margolies, ESTO; all others, Dale Howard.

Morris was more than a chair   Drawing from *William Morris Textiles* by Linda Parry (Weidenfeld and Nicolson, 1983).

Music for the eyes   Photograph, © 1988 The Art Institute of Chicago. All rights reserved.

Tools of the trade   Drawings, Stuart Armstrong.

Rise to great heights   p. 32, top left, Chicago Historical Society; top right, Irving Underhill, Museum of the City of New York; bottom left, Irving Browning, The New-York Historical Society; middle, Philip Johnson Collection; bottom right, © 1984 Richard Payne AIA. p. 33, drawing, Elsie Hennig, based on drawings in *Perspecta 18, The Yale Architectural Journal*, 1982. p. 34, Sears, Roebuck and Company. p. 35, drawing, David Owsiany and Elsie Hennig, based on drawings by The Ehrenkrantz Group, courtesy Joseph Grabowski, F. W. Woolworth Company.

Pieces of history   p. 36, Herbert H. Harwood, Jr. p. 37, photograph, Tomas Sennet; drawing, Elsie Hennig and Pamela Trible.

Dress up Queen Anne   p. 38–39, "Butterfield Tile" wallpaper reproduction, Cole and Son. p. 40–41, house drawing, Tracy Bond, based on drawing by Stephen Rynerson in *A Gift to the Street* by Carol Olwell and Judith Lynch Waldhorn (St. Martin's Press, 1976); other drawings, Tracy Bond.

Bring back Main Street   With thanks to Richard Wagner, AIA. p. 42–43, decorative brick sidewalk, Galesburg, Ill., Clarkson Shoettle. p. 44–45, new building drawings, David Owsiany; Main Street row from *Broad Street Old and Historic District, Richmond, Virginia: Guidelines and Standards* (Historic Richmond Foundation, 1986); photograph, Galesburg, Ill., Clarkson Shoettle collection.

Star signs   p. 46, courtesy Science Press, Ephrata, Pa.

How to spot a gargoyle   p. 50–51, Morton Broffman. p. 52, left, Cathaleen Curtiss, *The Washington Times*; right, Morton Broffman. p. 53, left, Morton Broffman; right, Byron Chambers. Masks, Elsie Hennig.

Wooden wonders   p. 54, Montague City Bridge, Montague City, Mass., Arthur C. Haskell, HABS. Bridge drawing, HABS.

Go build!   p. 61, drawings, Donald Gates. p. 62, 64, 66 and 68, detail from a floor plan for Decatur House, Washington, D.C., NTHP. p. 63, left to right by row, NTHP; National Park Service, Olmsted National Historic Site; Virginia State Library; National Park Service, Olmsted NHS; Houghton Library, Harvard University; Cervin Robinson, HABS; Marler, NTHP; Pennsylvania Railroad; Society for the Preservation of New England Antiquities (SPNEA); Sadin/Karant Photography; South Carolina Historical Society. p. 65, left to right by row, Glessner House Foundation; Stanford University; St. John's Church; Guggenheim Museum; Museum of the City of New York; John Blumenson, NTHP; Hedrich-Blessing; Hedrich-Blessing; Maryland Historical Society, Library of Congress; SPNEA; Hedrich-Blessing. p. 67, California Division of Beaches and Parks; Boston Atheneum; SPNEA; Hedrich-Blessing; Michael J. Cronin, University of Virginia; James H. Edelen; U.S. General Services Administration; Robert Thall, HABS; SPNEA; Jack Boucher, HABS; Documents Collection, College of Environmental Design, University of California, Berkeley.

Going to school in 1862   p. 69–74, illustrations based on drawings from Richard Bergmann Architects. p. 70, top, Richard Bergmann Architects; bottom, Lockwood House Collection. p. 71 and 73, horse and carriage drawings, Loel Barr. p. 75, *Snap the Whip* (1873), by Winslow Homer, *Harper's Weekly*, Library of Congress.

Light work   With thanks to James Hyland, Lighthouse Preservation Society. Drawings, Elsie Hennig.

Who'll save old No. 9?   With thanks to Rebecca Zurier's *The American Firehouse* (Abbeville Press, 1982). p. 78, hats, courtesy Sotheby's, Inc. p. 78 and 79, old Philadelphia firehouses, INA Corporation Museum. p. 83, P. S. Duval and Sons, Historical Society of Pennsylvania. Drawings, Elsie Hennig.

Answers

Building with nature   1. Sea urchin
2. Starfish 3. Four-leaf clover 4. Leaves
5. Sea gull 6. Fish scales 7. Nautilus
shell 8. Onions 9. Daisy

Who settled where?
SAVIANANDINSC: Scandinavians, Minnesota. CHEESIN: Chinese, California.
SPANHISIC: Hispanics, Texas. GLISHEN:
English, Virginia. RICANSAF: Africans,
Mississippi. SSURIANS: Russians, Alaska.
CHNERF: French, Louisiana. SMANGER:
Germans, Pennsylvania. CHUDT: Dutch,
New Jersey. NAMERICA SDINNIA: American Indians, Oklahoma.

Voices from the past   10, 12, 5, 11,
4, 15, 1, 14, 16, 13, 6, 3, 8, 9, 2, 7

History mystery   1. 90°F 2. Less
than 1″ 3. shrubs 4. factories 5. desert
6. western 7. boiler and furnace 8. ore
9. shrub branches 10. fuel for a fire
11. large wagon 12. blacksmith
13. horses or mules 14. water 15. borax
16. cook 17. clerk 18. 1886 19. China
20. California 21. work clothes
22. mining camp

How houses change   Roofing material changed. Skylight installed. Downspout added to gutters. Exterior color
changed. Architectural ornamentation
removed. Windows changed. Door replaced. Porch flooring changed. Indoor
plumbing replaced outhouse and pump.
Electricity replaced wood stoves and
kerosene lighting. Kitchen layout and
fixtures changed. Bedroom fixtures and
furnishings changed. Bedroom ceiling
opened up into attic. Barn became a
garage. Car replaced buggy. TV and
antenna added. Bathroom added. Washer and dryer replaced wash tub. Tree
grew and bushes added.

Picture this   Watered the plants.
Played the piano. Rocked a baby. Read a
book. Served tea. Set the grandfather
clock. Slid down the banister. Lighted
the lamps.

Block by block   Mel's Diner: Restaurant, Moderne, Metal, Plate glass, Curvilinear, Vent cap. Kuntz House: Home,
Victorian, Brick, 2-over-2, Side gable,
Lintel. Odd Fellows Hall: Meeting place,
Vernacular, Wood, Transom, End gable
(wood), Lunette. Grace Church: Church,
Gothic Revival, Stone, Stained glass, End
gable (stone), Bell tower.

A-mazing landmarks

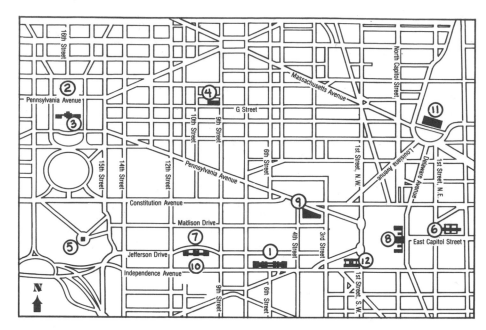

Down on the farm

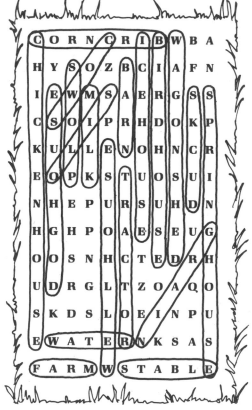

Watch out for ducks!   1. Tail o' the
Pup 2. Orange Julep 3. Bob's Java Jive
4. Benewah Dairy No. 1 5. Whale Car
Wash 6. Lucy the Elephant 7. Big Fish
Supper Club

What does your garden say?
"With gratitude and devotion on Mother's Day."

An architectural rebus   My great
grandparents' house was built in 1845.
It's in the Greek Revival style with stately
columns on the front, a triangular
pediment on top and a window which
lets sunlight into the attic. Each column
has a decorative carved capital. Over the
front door is a transom window. My
great grandpa's house is painted white
as snow and the shutters are black. Can
you name the parts of this Greek Revival
house?

I'm sign smart   1. Ice cream cone
2. The Shoe Box 3. Dentist 4. Cola
5. Flying horse 6. Antiques 7. Jonah and
the Whale 8. Disneyland 9. Hammer
Motel

Tools of the trade   Carpenters:
Wood, Build a staircase. Painters: Paint,
Paint a wall. Sculptors: Stone, Carve a
gargoyle. Metalsmiths: Tongs, Design a
railing. Plasterers: Decorative mold, Restore a molding. Weavers: Fabric, Make
curtains.

On Main Street   C or D

Bring back Main Street   3

Welcome to stencil craft   6, 8 and
10

Archi-venture   1. p. 72, Going to
school in 1862 2. p. 27, I'm sign smart
3. p. 12, History mystery 4. p. 9, Voices
from the past 5. p. 54, Wooden wonders 6. p. 65, Go build! 7. p. 44, Bring
back Main Street 8. p. 22, Watch out for
ducks! 9. p. 84, Who'll save old No. 9?
10. p. 31, Tools of the trade 11. p. 34,
Rise to great heights 12. p. 41, Dress up
Queen Anne 13. p. 4, Building with
nature 14. p. 77, Light work 15. p. 18,
Block by block 16. p. 46, Star signs